Love Your Work!

David L. McKenna

VICTOR BOOKS®

A DIVISION OF SCRIPTURE PRESS PUBLICATIONS INC.
USA CANADA ENGLAND

Scripture quotations, unless otherwise noted, are from *The New King James Version*, © 1979, 1980, 1982, Thomas Nelson, Inc., Publishers. Other quotations are from the *Holy Bible, New International Version* (NIV), © 1973, 1978, 1984, International Bible Society. Used by permission of Zondervan Bible Publishers.

Library of Congress Cataloging-in-Publication Data

McKenna, David L. (David Loren), 1929–
  Love your work! / by David L. McKenna.
    p.   cm.
  Includes bibliographical references.
  ISBN 0-89693-036-X
  1. Work—Religious aspects—Christianity. I. Title.
BT738.5.M57   1990
241.64–dc20   90-12127
                                                                CIP

1 2 3 4 5 6 7 8 9 10 Printing/Year 94 93 92 91 90

CONTENTS

To
JANET
My wife of forty years
whose daily work
as the President's First Lady
for thirty years
is
her work of faith,
her labor of love,
and
my inspiration of hope
in Jesus Christ

FOREWORD

This Spiritual Formation book is for the Christian who hears God's call to a devotional life, and wants to better serve Him in the challenges of every day. It draws on the richness of Christian spirituality through the centuries of church history, but with an application to the twentieth-century believer who is involved in society, rather than withdrawn from it.

Spiritual formation blends the best of traditional discipleship concepts with the more reflective disciplines of an individual journey toward friendship with God. It is a lifestyle, not a program; a relationship rather than a system; a journey instead of a road map. It calls us into holy partnership with God for our spiritual development.

As you read this book, and then others in the series, I hope that you will receive much more than information. My prayer is that you will experience new levels of formation of your mind and heart, and find yourself drawn closer to Christ.

Steven Harper, General Editor
Associate Professor of Spiritual Formation
Asbury Theological Seminary

PREFACE

As a seminary president, I have had my share of honors. None, however, is more gratifying than to be asked to be part of a faculty writing team on the subject of "spirituality." The honor suggests that I have something to say on the subject. More than that, the writing project joins us together as President and Faculty in communicating what I consider the "heartbeat" of Asbury Theological Seminary.

Long before "spiritual formation" spread through seminary education with the excitement of a new discovery, Asbury had the emphasis upon prayer and spirituality as integral to our life and learning. In fact, under the leadership of Dr. Thomas Carruth, we pioneered with an academic Department of Prayer and Spiritual Life.

Our heritage in spirituality has its roots in the doctrine and experience of "scriptural holiness." In our Wesleyan heritage, in our chartered purpose, and in our history of spiritual revival, scriptural holiness is identified as the reason for our existence. Specifically, we are referring to a quality of life created in us by the cleansing, filling, and empowering work of the Holy Spirit and leading to the discipline and the doing of holy living, both personally and socially. The Wesleys expressed the meaning of scriptural holiness best when they spoke of "faith working through love." So it is that the spirituality of "being" and "doing" beat as one pulse at Asbury.

Our daily work has to be one of the critical areas of contemporary life where our spirituality is tested. Yet, the spirituality of work is a neglected subject about an activity that absorbs more than eighty percent of our waking hours. The single purpose of this book is to put the "being" and "doing" dilemmas of the modern workplace into biblical perspective.

Special thanks are due to Dr. Steve Harper, who initiated the Spiritual Formation Series and serves as General Editor; to my faculty colleagues in writing, Drs. Donald Joy, Reginald Johnson, Jerry Mercer, and Donald Demaray; to Carole Streeter, Editor of Victor Books who prompted and prodded us; and to Sheila Lovell and Lois Mulcahy, the ever patient and always encouraging editorial-production team in my office.

David L. McKenna, President
Asbury Theological Seminary
Wilmore, Kentucky
1990

ONE

OUR DAILY WORK: A SPIRITUAL RESOURCE

*L*abor is "the lost province of Christian faith."

—Elton Trueblood

Do you hate to get up and go to work on Monday morning? Do you wish that you could work at something else? Do you suffer physical, emotional, or spiritual symptoms from job stress?

Each of us has mornings when we would answer a resounding "Yes!" to these questions. Even pastors, teachers, counselors, evangelists, and missionaries have their down days. Saints through the ages have confessed to periods of deep and prolonged depression, best described by St. John of the Cross as the "dark night of the soul."[1]

Yesterday's mail included a copy of a letter from a disillusioned young professor who teaches religion in a Christian college. Writing to a friend who had left Christian higher education for a secular field of work, he vented his frustration about a "foot-dragging administration" which blocked one of his creative proposals. He closed the letter with the bitter words, "I'm even finding it hard to pray. Aren't you glad that you are out of Christian higher education?"

His disillusionment reminds us that our work directly affects our spiritual outlook. We can also say that our spiritual outlook affects our work. After a long and torturous ride, a circuit rider arrived at a village to hold a revival meeting. Totally fatigued, he wrote in his journal just before collapsing into bed, "There will be no revival here. The people are not ready and the Spirit is not present." The next morning, however, he awakened from a good night of sleep to be greeted by a sumptuous country breakfast. Prayers with the family followed the meal. When the circuit rider returned to his room he made a new entry into his journal which read, "Revival is on the way. The people are ready and I can already sense the moving of the Spirit." It is amazing what a good night of sleep and a hearty meal do for our spiritual outlook as well as for our work.

What does our work have to do with our spirituality? For most of us, our spirituality is connected with prayer, Bible study, fasting, and worship. Work is something else. Give the average person a word association test in which he or she is asked to say the first word that comes to mind when you mention *work*. The initial responses are "hassle," "duty," "paycheck," "time clock," "sweat," and "drudgery." Second thoughts usually reveal a more positive attitude toward work with words such as "reward," "challenge," and "excitement."

Seldom, however, are the words "love," "ministry," "meaning," and "joy" associated with our work. Especially when we think about our spiritual growth, work is put into a world of its own. Secular work, in particular, is separated from our spirituality and is seen as either a testing ground for our faith or a begrudging sidestep on our spiritual journey. Something is wrong. If we believe that our spiritual development encompasses the whole of life, why is our daily work so often considered an eight-hour interruption in our growth?

A TWO-STORY THEOLOGY OF WORK

Throughout the history of the Christian church, the relationship between spirituality and work has been one of debate, confusion, and neglect. Early in Christian history, monks fled to the desert away from the contamination of the world to pursue spirituality through contemplation, self-denial, and hard labor. Later, in the Middle Ages, the theology of the church sliced all of the world horizontally into two distinct layers—the sacred and the profane. According to this split-world view, any activity which took place in the church was "sacred." All other activities which went on outside the church or in the marketplace were downgraded as "profane."

In their book, *Your Work Matters to God*, Sherman and Hendricks identify this attitude as the "two-story view of work." The top floor is occupied by "sacred" work with "secular" work underneath. This two-story world is built upon the unbiblical assumption that the "soul is over the body, the eternal is over the temporal, and the clergy are over the laity."[2] If the two-story view of work is true, our goal in life should be to escape secular work and seek spiritual work—as soon as possible.

This is just what happened in the early history of the church. A stratified theology of work created a spiritual caste system with priests who ministered in the church being recognized as superior to the people who labored in the marketplace. While we may reject such a theology as unbiblical, the tension still remains between spiritual ministries and secular careers. When I was a boy, a missionary speaker made a lasting impression on me when he jabbed his index finger into my chest and uttered the command, "God is calling you to be a missionary. Anything else is second-best!"

Luther, in the theology of the Reformation, worked to repair the split-world theology of work. When he stood his ground at the Diet of Worms and declared, "Here I stand. I can do no other. So help me God!" Luther challenged the power of the priesthood and its stranglehold on spirituality. By this act, he also reconnected the world of work with the world of spirituality. In his classic writings on Christian vocation, Luther left no doubt that the "priesthood of believers" is one side of the Reformation coin; the other side is the "sacredness of all callings," including secular work.

In the ensuing centuries, work has again become separated from spirituality, perhaps not in doctrine, but certainly in practice. The workplace is one of the most sensitive centers for changing values in our society. Beginning with the Enlightenment of the seventeenth century and advancing into the scientific movement of the nineteenth century, work has been increasingly identified as a rational and specialized process independent of spiritual meaning. Add to the march of history the Industrial Revolution in the nineteenth century, with the development of megascale corporations, and then step up the pace to double time with the complexities of the computerized world in the twentieth century. Specialization has taken over the workplace, leaving spirituality as an independent area of its own expertise.

As if all of these forces which have driven a deep wedge between work and spirituality were not enough, we are now living with a full dose of self-interest in our attitude toward work. Little or no contradiction is seen between developing spiritual resources away from the job, but not on the job. Off the job, our spiritual goals may be self-denial, self-discipline, and self-sacrifice; but on the job, our personal goals are just the opposite—security, status, success, and most of all, self-satisfaction. A prominent chief executive of one of our most profitable international corporations spoke with brutal honesty when he said, "On Sunday, my priorities are God, family, and business. On Monday morning, they are all reversed."

Little help has come from the church in developing a life-encompassing biblical theology of work. One reason for this failure is the speed of social change which keeps the workplace in constant flux. Within just a century, we have passed with dizzying speed from the Age of Agriculture, through the Age of

Industry and into the Age of Information. Our doctrine of spiritual work, however, is stuck in the Age of Agriculture when the farmer labored close to nature, worked alone or with his extended family, and lived intimately with the product of his work from beginning to end. When we compare the farmer with the factory worker who deals with pre-made materials, and participates in just a small part of the total process, we can understand how our theology of work foundered in the factory. While the church was failing to develop a biblical view of work for the Age of Industry, labor unions stepped in with a philosophy of their own that leaned left and caused conservative Christians to flee back into the sanctuary of their split-world view. They were tempted more than ever to secularize their daily work and spiritualize their daily devotions.

The Age of Information has further isolated the worker from nature, from other workers, and from the finished product. Computer systems have brought a radical shift of power from hand to brain, from physical energy to intellectual energy, and from the wealth of money to the wealth of information. A whole generation of workers is adversely affected. They either fall out of the system as the unemployed people of our times or stay in the system as the underemployed victims of the Age of Information. Repeated statistics bear out these sobering facts:

Eighty percent of all Americans hate to get out of bed and go to work on Monday morning.

A majority of all Americans wish that they could work at something else.

Twenty-five percent of all Americans suffer severe symptoms of job stress, such as absenteeism, substance abuse, divorce, physical illness, and poor quality of work.

Caught in the gears of the changing workplace, Christians too can be ground up by the shifting system. On any given Sunday, there are worshipers in our churches who are unemployed, underemployed, changing jobs, and living with stress from the workplace. Negative attitudes toward their work are affecting their physical and mental health, their self-esteem, and their family relations; they cannot help but also adversely affect their spiritual well-being. Yet, the spiritual meaning of work is addressed in few churches. For the most part, the person in the pew has to fashion a theology of work from one of two extremes: Work as a curse or work as a savior.

WORK AS A CURSE

Like an infected appendix which we don't need, a doctrine of the past which makes work a curse for our sin continues to afflict us. The idea comes from a wrongheaded interpretation of God's sentence upon Adam and Eve for their sin:

> Cursed is the ground for your sake;
>   In toil you shall eat of it all the days of your life.
>
> Both thorns and thistles it shall bring forth for
>   you,
> And you shall eat the herb of the field.
>
> In the sweat of your face you shall eat bread
>   till you return to the ground.
> For dust you are, and to dust you shall return
>   (Genesis 3:17b-19).

A more exact translation of the first line of this passage is, "Condemned is the ground on your account." The earth itself is a reminder that all creation is affected by our sin. And make no mistake, the resistance of nature makes work hard. Our failure to come to grips with the reality of an earth that requires the hard work of both "tending and taming," as God command- ed its first inhabitants, is now catching up with us. Breaking its precedent for naming a person as its "Man of the Year," *Time* magazine gave the award to Planet Earth in 1988 with a warning that our wondrous globe is due for disaster unless we abandon our reckless ways and do something about our overpopulation, pollution, waste of resources, and wanton destruction of natural habitats. The curse of sin is within us and all creation, including our work, can become its own victim.

Still, we persist in treating work as though it were a curse in itself. In his classic book *Working*, Studs Terkel puts the sting of the curse on his subject, "This book, being about work, is by its very nature, about violence."[3] Terkel came to this con- clusion after interviewing hundreds of working Americans across the nation. Most felt as if their jobs symbolized a form of Monday through Friday dying.[4] Behind their morbid descrip- tions lurks the notion that work is a curse with which we must live—a curse that beats us down, wears us out, robs us of our dignity, and serves us right. Terkel concluded that most of the people he met felt condemned to the curse of working on jobs that were "too small for their spirits."[5] A brilliant friend of mine dropped out of college and spent thirty years working on a repetitious but skilled job only to be rendered obsolete by com- puter technology. After an insufferable period of unemploy- ment, he took a job on a loading dock at less than half the wages of his former employment. Dropping his head in shame, he confessed to me, "I guess I don't deserve any better." He seems to see his daily work as a curse for his sin or a fitting punishment for his unworthiness.

Whether or not we buy into the false theology of work as a curse, we still put it into practice in various ways. One way is *to perpetuate the attitude that some callings are sacred and others are secular.* How well I remember my first confrontation with this viewpoint. After graduation from Asbury Theological Seminary, I accepted the call to teach in a Christian college. Returning home, I was met on the front porch by a saintly sister in our home church, who wrapped me in her she-bear arms and wept, "Oh, oh, oh, I had prayed so hard that God would call you into ministry!" To her the call to preach not only stood above the call to teach—it also stood spiritually separate. At the time I answered nothing. Today I would be tempted to ask if she had ever put the question to her husband, a prominent and affluent CPA, "Why didn't God call you into ministry?"

Another way in which we keep the doctrine of the curse alive is *to create a spiritual hierarchy among our sacred callings.* Nine months before my encounter on the front porch with the woman who had prayed for me, my denominational adviser at the seminary asked me to come into his office. He began by explaining, "To retain your scholarship at the seminary, you must declare that you will take a pastorate after graduation." To be honest, I had to answer, "God has called me into ministry, but whether it is preaching or teaching, I'm not sure." My answer cost me the scholarship. Twenty-nine years later, I returned to the seminary as president, after a career in Christian higher education. Now in moments of jest, I remind church leaders that they owe me a retroactive grant. This episode makes a strong point when I talk to students about the meaning of ministry. The error of separating the sacred from the secular in our work is compounded when we create within our sacred callings a hierarchy of ministries.

Still another way in which we express an unbiblical view of work is *to use our daily work as a secular means to a spiritual end.* I recently reviewed a book that used the Apostle Paul's tentmaking as the Christian's model for work. Claiming the authority of Scripture, the author said that all Christians must be tentmakers, using their secular employment as the means that frees them for spiritual ministry. Moreover, the author contended that conversion will cause many Christians to change jobs, as Paul did, so that they can go into evangelism. This author is wrong. Paul's tentmaking, according to his own words, served a special purpose for his apostleship (1 Thessalonians 2:9). True, his tentmaking gave him credibility in the secular city, but its major purpose was to free him to preach the whole Gospel. He feared that if he depended on someone else for support, he might ease up on the truth.

This model is certainly applicable to our day when evangelists are living in luxury from the sacrificial gifts of believers, and when large donors may influence the direction of a ministry. But Paul makes no claim that we should all be tentmakers in order to preach the Gospel. To the contrary, we find a case in Paul's tentmaking for the spirituality of our daily work. According to Scripture, Paul pursued his craft months at a time, thereby opening himself to the charge of misplaced priorities in the light of the size of the need and the shortness of time that he had to preach the Gospel. His daily work of tentmaking, then, had to have meaning in itself.

As for the idea of changing jobs when we are converted, Paul reaches quite a different verdict. Although we who live in a democracy are quick to criticize him, he tells those who are in slavery to be content with their position unless the opportunity for freedom comes to them (1 Corinthians 7:21-24). Rather than advocating that we change employment upon conversion, Paul puts higher value on being content and finding meaning in the job we have. To remain on the job after conversion may well give us the greatest test of faith and the greatest opportunity for witness.

An auto dealer who sold Jaguars once told me, "Selling cars is my business; witnessing is my life." By this he meant that he worked to become independently wealthy so that he could be free for Christian evangelism. Certainly the motive sounds good and the goal seems worthy. To his credit, when he made a fortune, he remained true to his promise. Selling cars on a twenty-hour week, he spent the rest of his time traveling as a lay evangelist.

Perhaps I am wrong, but I wonder if his view of secular work discourages those of us who will never be independently wealthy and will have to work a forty-hour week until the day we retire. Frankly, I also wonder about buying a car from him, now that he is free to spend one-half of his time in evangelism. Because my father worked as an automotive engineer in quality control, I grew up in the shadow of Detroit when it was the undisputed auto capital of the world. I expect quality in both sales and service for my cars. I don't want a car dealer looking over his shoulder at his sacred work when he sells me a car, or giving me less than his full attention when I bring it in for service. Someone once said, "When I need an operation, I want the best surgeon, Christian or not." Somehow I feel the same way about service on my automobile. I want an auto dealer whose secular work in sales and service is a spiritual ministry in itself. Otherwise, I am never sure when the inferior position of secular work might show up as inferior performance on my automobile. Wherever the two-story view of work shows itself, the shadow of the curse is seen.

To view work as a curse, then, necessitates that we separate it from the totality of life. If work is violent, we must hate it; if sacred work is superior to secular work, we must seek the one and escape the other; if work is punishment for sin, we must pay the price. In each and every case, the hex remains.

WORK AS A SAVIOR

At the other extreme, work is viewed as a savior. In other words, work can become a god in itself. The other day I heard a Christian businesswoman say, "If someone wants to visit me, let them come to my office. After all, it's my home." Whether she meant it or not, she conveyed the idea that her work had moved to the center of her life. Such a view of work may heal the breach between the sacred and the secular, but the danger is that work becomes so all-possessing that it also is a substitute savior. The even greater danger is that work which becomes a self-centered, self-contained, and self-glorifying end in itself, promising to be a savior, ends up as a demon.

Marxism is built upon the premise that work is a savior—the highest good of human behavior. Without a belief in God, sin, or redemption, Marxists put the person in place of God, condemn sloth as a sin, and make work the way of redemption. Immediately, we see the difference between Capitalism and Communism. Capitalism elevates the accumulation of wealth as the highest economic good, while Communism raises the productivity of work to the highest social good. While neither philosophy is Christian, Capitalism does not rule out Christianity; Communism does. Even now the convulsions in the Communist world condemn a totalitarian system that puts productivity above people. The inherent human drive for freedom—political, economic, and religious—can be stifled only so long. To make work the savior of human dignity is a false premise which has now been exposed. Communism, not capitalism, is ready for burial.

In the West, our danger is making work a savior in terms of radical self-interest. Along with our economic affluence, we have adopted the attitude of entitlement which says, "The world owes me a living." Observers sum up the decade of the '80s in one word, *Greed*. We expect our work to give us not just financial rewards to guarantee our high standard of living, but also the satisfaction of self-fulfillment. In his book *New Rules: Living in a World Turned Upside Down*, Daniel Yankelovich puts it this way: "We expect more of everything."[6] Studies of our contemporary attitude toward work confirm this.

In *Habits of the Heart*, Robert Bellah wrote that the prevailing attitudes among the younger generation are "expressive" and "utilitarian" self-interest.[7] Expressive self-interest is the expectation that *we can be what we want to be;* utilitarian self-interest is *the demand to do what we want to do.* Our work, then, is judged by the standards of self-interest. It is not enough for our daily work to be the means for meeting our basic needs for food, clothing, and shelter, or even our added desires for security, status, and success. We expect our work to be self-actualizing and self-fulfilling. Not by accident, the terms *self-actualization* and *self-fulfillment* have become substitutes for *redemption* and *salvation.* In other words, the sometimes celebrated and often maligned Protestant work ethic of the past, which emphasized industry and prosperity, has given way to the demands for self-satisfaction and self-realization. Strange as it seems, a love-hate relationship exists within the working world today. At the same time that we condemn technical work as depersonalizing, we espouse ever higher expectations for our work. The workplace is regarded as a sanctuary in which work itself becomes a god, the worker a communicant, and work relationships the redemptive community.

To view work as a savior, then, is to create an idolatry which is abominable to God. If work is our highest good, we need no other treasure; if work is the means for our salvation, we need no other savior; if the workplace is our sanctuary, we need no other church. To avoid the idolatry of work, we must rediscover its biblical meaning.

WORK AS A MEANS OF GRACE

If work is neither curse nor savior, what is it? To reconnect our daily work with biblical spirituality, we must see work as a resource of creation waiting to be redeemed by those who believe. Once redeemed it becomes a means of grace. For a start, ask yourself these questions:

Do you feel called of God to the work you do?
Do you believe that your daily work develops
   the special gifts that God has given you?
Do you feel as if your daily work is contributing
   to your spiritual growth?
Do you believe that your daily work is contrib-
   uting to the moral good of your community?
   To the body of Christ? To the kingdom of
   God?
Do you see the results of your daily work as
   glorifying God?

I didn't know it was Katie kneeling in the flower bed
next to where I parked my car. A red bandana covered her
head, overalls enveloped her body, hiking boots encased her
feet, and Green Thumb gloves protected her hands. As I opened
the car door, I said, "Hello." Katie returned the greeting by
surprising me with a smile I recognized.

"Didn't you just graduate from the university?" I asked.

"Yes," Katie answered, "I majored in English literature
and you gave me my degree."

"Then what are you doing in the flower bed?" I blurted.

Katie smiled again without embarrassment. "Waiting for
a teaching job to open up."

"Oh," I continued with my foot in my mouth. "You're in
the ranks of the underemployed?"

"No," Katie corrected me, "I'm learning landscaping
while I wait. I love my work."

How would Katie answer the questions about the spirituality of her daily work? She illustrates the Christian in vocation—responding to the call of God, discovering her special
gifts, making her job big enough for her soul, relating her work
to the meaning of life, and discovering joy in the process. What
she discovered, we want to learn.

SPIRITUAL REFLECTIONS ON OUR DAILY WORK

The creation itself also will be delivered
from the bondage of corruption into the
glorious liberty of the children of God.

Romans 8:21

A PROVOCATIVE QUESTION

Do you hate to get up and go to work on Monday morning? Do you
wish that you could work at something else? Do you suffer from the
symptoms of job stress?

If you answered "Yes" to any of these questions, what is the effect
upon your spiritual life? Do you pray about these problems? Have you
sought spiritual counsel? Have you searched the Word of God with
these questions in mind?

A PRACTICAL EXERCISE

What is the relationship between your faith and your daily work? Have
you made work a curse or a savior? How can it become a means of
grace?

A PERSONAL PRAYER

Lord, teach me the spiritual meaning of my daily work. If I have made
it a curse or a savior, forgive me. From this day forward, may I begin
to discover my daily work as a means of Your grace. Amen

T W O

OUR CURRENT DILEMMA: THE CHANGING WORKPLACE

*T*ake This Job and Shove It"
—Title of a popular song

Our spirituality is reflected in our character. But what is the connection between our character and our daily work? In the split-world view, there is no connection. If work is a curse, we must develop our character outside of our work. If work is a savior, then we will be more interested in self-fulfillment than in character building.

In its original meaning, the word *character* is synonymous with *imprint*. Long ago, noblemen attested their agreements by pressing the imprint of their signet rings into a seal of wax. Their mark stood for the integrity of their character and served as their bond.

Gail Sheehy, in her best-selling book, *Character: America's Search for Leadership,*[1] follows this idea by tracing the biographical imprint from the lives of six candidates for the United States presidency in 1988, and from that imprint, infers their character. There is a predictability of character based upon the imprint of personal history. Although we see redemptive exceptions, Sheehy's book gives us the general rule: past integrity is the best predictor of future integrity.

When we think about the development of Christian character, we emphasize the imprinting influence to spiritual experience. Of course, we put the highest premium upon "born again" as being the essence of character development. To that experience, we add the influence of being "filled with the Spirit," the nurture of our spiritual discipline, the relational support of the body of Christ, and the honing of social holiness in deeds of justice, mercy, and love. Little attention, however, is given to a changing culture which also shapes our character and influences our spirituality.

The world of work is a foremost example. Students of our culture read changes in the workplace like a barometer on a national character. Michael Maccoby, author of *The Gamesman* and *Leader*, writes: "It is in the workplace that social and national characters are normally forged and new models of leadership are most often tested."[2]

If Maccoby is right, then what are the far-reaching implications of Studs Terkel's discovery that most Americans are working on jobs that are "too small for their spirits"? More specifically, how does a changing workplace imprint our character and influence our spirituality?

THE CHANGING WORKPLACE

Our traditional ideas about the nature of work are being turned upside down today. Most evident is *the decline of heavy industry* with its dependence upon the human resources of semiskilled labor and the physical resources of steel, oil, and coal. The implications are far-reaching. Unemployment in heavy industry lines runs high and there is no promise that the workers will be rehired. Labor unions, which gained by organizing workers in heavy industry, are struggling to stay alive. Of necessity their negotiations are shifting from guaranteed employment to guaranteed retraining.

Paralleling the decline in heavy industry is *the spectacular rise of high technology* with its lightning-fast hardware and its ingenious software. High tech has literally taken over the workplace. Early in the 1980s, the majority of expenditures in our gross national product shifted from the "heavy" industries of manufacturing to the "light" industries of information and communication. Of course, the implications for the nature of our daily work are nothing short of revolutionary. Information and communication industries run on brains, not fossil fuels; they work with ideas, not raw materials; and they demand sophisticated intellectual skills, not manual labor.

Still another change in the American workplace is *the number of women on the job*. Not only is the number of women working outside the home at an all-time high, but for the first time a majority of mothers are employed. Time will tell how women in the workplace will change the nature of work and how working mothers will affect the structure of the family. At present, we know that women are striving for equal pay and status on the job. As they do, they show the stress symptoms of upward mobility. Also, as they climb the organizational ladder to top level positions, they meet men coming down the ladder because executive status and success have failed to bring them satisfaction.

THE TRAUMA OF CHANGE

While the trends of the changing workplace are societal, the resulting trauma is personal. We may sigh when we read the statistics of unemployment, but our souls are shaken to the core when we hear the stories of displaced, dislocated, disillusioned, and distressed workers.

Displaced workers are persons whose life skills are now obsolete. Typical is a fifty-five-year-old employee of the automobile industry, who lost his job on the assembly line. He spoke so pitifully, "I'm too young to die and too old to learn a new trade." The future bodes no better. It is predicted that young persons entering the job market today will change careers three or four times during a lifetime, due to changes in the nature of work. Retraining will become standard, not just for skilled labor, but for professional persons as well. The need for skilled labor will change as technology expands; the need for professionals will fluctuate as fields such as law, business, and medicine are saturated.

Dislocated workers are persons who have lived and worked for a lifetime in a "company town." Then, the industry cuts back or shuts down, leaving them no alternative but to move, go on unemployment, or create a new job for themselves. When the Boeing Aircraft Company lost the SST contract in 1969 and laid off 60,000 workers, a billboard appeared at the edge of the town reading:

"WILL THE LAST ONE TO LEAVE
PLEASE TURN OUT THE LIGHTS!"

This billboard could have been erected at the city limits of hundreds of company towns across the country. With escalating costs at home and cheap labor abroad, American industry has shifted much of its business overseas to remain competitive. Controversial legislation has been enacted requiring a company to give prior notice of a move and compensation for the displaced worker. But the trauma remains. Many workers cannot move, others cannot be retrained, and all suffer the loss of meaningful work, which is vital to human dignity.

Disillusioned workers are people on the job who have lost the vision for their work. We have already noted the eighty percent of Americans who hate to get up and go to work on Monday morning, a majority who wish that they could work at something else, and one-quarter who suffer from severe symptoms of job stress. Another survey shows that fifty percent of public school teachers admit that they are "dead-ended" and "burned out."

Management usually gets the blame for disillusioned workers. Bosses who offer the privilege of employee participation in management decisions are usually cited as antidotes for disillusionment. Little is said about the changing nature of the workplace or the value of the work itself. Public school teachers will tell you that the conditions for learning have changed drastically, especially in urban schools, which are plagued by students who come from drug- and crime-ridden areas without parental support or motivation for schooling.

In yet another sphere, seminary enrollments are being sustained by "second-career seminarians." By and large, these students are Christians who have pursued a secular career for ten years or more and achieved satisfactions of salary, security, and success. Some may have been running from the call to ministry, but most have been called out of their secular professions to prepare for ordination. They too might be listed among the disillusioned workers, but their disillusionment was not frustration or failure in their work. Rather, they realized that the rewards of their secular professions did not satisfy their spiritual longings. Literally, they want to give themselves away, and they do. To resign from a job, give up a salary, sell a home, move one's family, and enter intensive graduate study is a sacrifice similar to that made by Abraham, who went out from Haran under the call of God, "not knowing where he was going" (Hebrews 11:8). One might argue that second-career seminarians are victims of the split-world view, which makes a secular career spiritually inferior to the ordained ministry. Knowing these students as I do, I think not. The truth of the matter is that radical self-interest has so captured the aspirations of Christian students today that the number opting for the ordained ministry and seminary education immediately after college is very low. This is especially true for the best and the brightest of our college graduates. Nothing is wrong with the careers they choose, but they choose them for the wrong reasons.

Students at evangelical Christian colleges, for example, place high value on the goal of self-realization, according to

James Davison Hunter, in his book *Evangelicalism: The Coming Generation.*[3] Again, nothing is wrong with self-realization, if it is grounded in the truth that it cannot be gained outside the will of God and the redeeming grace of Jesus Christ. As a longtime college president, I have witnessed the conflicts which our students face. They try to balance the psychological subtleties of self-realization with the call of Christ for self-sacrifice. They are dissatisfied with the dead end of affluence that they see in adults, but they still struggle against the natural desire to be successful, secure, and satisfied in a career which the culture rewards. Hence, they forsake the liberal arts as well as philosophy and religion to choose professional majors which lead directly to a "cash career." The issue is not a matter of a sacred/secular choice. Rather it is the motivation of self-realization versus self-sacrifice. Later, seeing for themselves the disillusion of self-realization, they respond to the call of God. In contrast with their counterparts who are disillusioned by the nature or conditions of their work, their disillusionment is related to the motive, the value, and the goal of their work.

Distressed workers are victims of the most severe kind of work-related trauma. High-stress jobs are those in which the employee is faced with exacting psychological demands over which he or she has no control. In fact, the formula for job stress can be written $S = \dfrac{D}{C}$.

Stress equals *demand* over *control*. Air controllers are reputed to be persons in high-stress jobs. The psychological demand is very high at the same time that there are so many factors out of their control. The stress equation for college professors is just the opposite. While the psychological demand of their work is relatively low, at least from external sources, they also have a high degree of freedom and control over those demands. Of course, whatever our work, our own psychological makeup will be a factor in raising and lowering our perception of these demands. Some people handle stress with ease. Some people carry undue stress with them. For example, on a simple task of low demand with high control, a perfectionist might raise the demand unrealistically and thus generate crippling stress.

One out of four Americans is job-distressed. They also live daily with the debilitating symptoms of absenteeism, heart disease, substance abuse, divorce, or broken relationships. If the economic losses to the employer are added to the social costs of such symptoms, billions of dollars are lost to distressed workers every year. Families, however, pay the greatest cost. Studies of trends among working parents are revealing that day-care centers, latchkey kids, family-crisis clinics, and help for troubled youth are highest in priority. Without doubt, provision for day-care services for working parents will be at the center of public domain in the decade of the 1990s. Whether the need will be met by government voucher or as a fringe benefit in private business, it must be regarded as a dramatic consequence of the changing workplace.

Changes in the workplace will be yet more traumatic in the future. Shudders run up and down the spine at the thought of a nation divided between the "haves" who hold the limited number of high-tech jobs and the "have-nots" who labor in the service and support force at lower pay. Competition for lower-level jobs will be fierce among single-parent women, ethnic minorities, senior citizens, youth, and downwardly mobile men. Ironically, just at the time when women are winning equal pay for equal work, changes in the nature of the workplace may force them down. The economic results are already evident. Statistics on unemployment and poverty show a widening gap between the rich and the poor. The bottom is dropping out of the lower-middle class as blue-collar workers are displaced by technology; and the bottom is being swelled by the ranks of unskilled and semiskilled women, ethnics, and elderly citizens who are becoming the "new poor" in our wealthy western world.

THE FUTURE OF WORK

What of the future? *First, we can expect the dehumanization of the workplace to continue.* The threat that the Industrial Revolution brought upon workers whose skilled hands were replaced by automation will be magnified in the Age of Information when the skills of the brain are replaced by computers. High-tech work will call out the need for high-touch churches. Relational theology will have to come of age in the biblical doctrine of holiness, as spelled out in the dimensions of personal and social wholeness. Likewise, the cardinal doctrines of Creation, the Fall, and Redemption will have to come together in a biblical doctrine of work.

Second, the occupational gap between the "haves" and "have-nots" will continue to widen. A shrinking middle class and an ever-widening gap between the rich and the poor are frightening trends that also threaten the church. Growing congregations whose success is based upon compatibility in education, income, status, and color are already an embarrassment to us. As the occupational, economic, and social gap between the "haves" and "have-nots" widens, will the spiritual gap also widen? The church must gear up now to close that gap.

Third, the psychology of the changing workplace will produce new symptoms of distress among workers. In addition to aggravating the symptoms of displacement, disillusionment, and distress among workers, the Age of Information will have its own work-related ailments. Loneliness was relatively unknown until the rise of the industrial age when mechanization broke down the social support of the village, the home, and the church. Loneliness became a plague that continues to spread among us. Susan Gordon identifies loneliness as a characteristic of the new American character.[4]

Add to this the threat of a computer-regulated life, just at the time when the social supports of the home, the church, and the school are crumbling. What symptoms will follow? Alienation? Loneliness? Or will it be ennui—the loss of human meaning which will speed the dehumanized worker into drugs, therapy, cults, and ecstatic religions? The "sanctity of the person" may well join the "sanctity of life" as one of the most crucial issues for our Brave New World in the twenty-first century. Right in the middle of these issues is our question, "What is the spirituality of work?"

† SPIRITUAL REFLECTIONS ON OUR CHANGING WORKPLACE

And whatever you do in word or deed, do
all in the name of the Lord Jesus, giving
thanks to God the Father through Him.
Colossians 3:17

A PROVOCATIVE QUESTION

Have you ever suffered from job stress? What symptom or symptoms
caused you the most difficulty? How did the stress affect your personal
relationships, especially with friends and family? How did you
recover?

A PRACTICAL EXERCISE

We have support groups in the church for many personal and interpersonal problems. Why not a support group for persons who are displaced, dislocated, disillusioned, or distressed in their work? Or, more
positively, a group of persons who are interested in discussing, "Spirituality and Daily Work"? What would be the goals for the group and
the agenda for the first meeting?

PERSONAL PRAYER

O Christ, may my soul grow large and may my daily work grow with
it. Amen

THREE

OUR BIBLICAL ETHIC: PARTNERS IN CREATION

*T*o THOMAS COBB

Who mended shoes

In this village

For forty years

TO THE GLORY OF GOD

—Epitaph on a tombstone

Because we Christians have failed to develop a biblical ethic for work, others have set the standard for us. In American history, we can trace an evolving work ethic which has moved farther and farther away from our biblical roots. We tend to react to these secularized ethics after the fact, but not until their influence is ingrained in the attitudes and values of our national character. A quick review of our evolving work ethic will not only help us understand what is happening to our national character, but may also prod us to the urgent task of developing a biblical ethic which sets our daily work in a spiritual context.

EVOLUTION OF AN ETHIC

Author Michael Maccoby traces five stages of the evolution of our work ethic in the course of American history.[1]

† First is the well-known and oft-disputed *Puritan Ethic*

which dominated Colonial times. Rooted in Calvinist theology, the motive for work was a sense of "vocation" or divine calling. With that motive our Puritan forefathers disciplined their lives and gave obedient service to their jobs. Most often, the nature of work in Colonial times represented a contest with the forces of nature on a small farm. Hard work equaled a holy task and responsibility, for success or failure depended upon divine will. Spurred on by the promise of God's blessing as the reward for their labor, the Puritans lived a simple, frugal, and reverent life in order to both survive and thrive. But the larger goal for their work involved more than personal prosperity. They also accepted the responsibility for contributing to the physical, moral, and spiritual quality of life in the community of faith and, in so doing, sought to glorify God. Perhaps John Wesley summed up the values of the Puritan Work Ethic when he advised, "Make all you can, save all you can, and give all you can."

† As time went on and the Colonies formed a nation, the celebrated Puritan Ethic gave way to the *Craftsman Ethic* of work in the era of Benjamin Franklin. *Poor Richard's Almanac* became the bible for the new ethic, with its shifting emphasis from the productive and communal Puritan to the creative and independent Craftsman. A distant deity still endowed persons with the gifts for work, but the motive and control now belonged to the individual. Rather than being dependent upon a sovereign God and engaging in work as a sacred calling, Poor Richard relied upon his own skills, thrift, and industry to win his way in the world. Subtly but definitively, Benjamin Franklin moved from a biblical to a humanized theology of work that was expressed in the adage of the Craftsman, "Early to bed, early to rise, makes a man healthy, wealthy, and wise."

† With the coming of the Industrial Revolution in the nineteenth century, the guiding ethic of work changed again. Maccoby identifies this change as the *Entrepreneurial Ethic* with the "jungle fighter" as its hero. Others have been less kind in their

description of the heroes for this ethic. Cornelius Vanderbilt, J.P. Morgan, John D. Rockefeller, and Andrew Carnegie still bear the derisive title of "Robber Barons" in the rising industrial state. According to their critics, greed dominated their motives for work as they clawed their way upward over the bodies and through the blood of their economic victims. In any case, the independence of the Craftsmen gave way to dog-eat-dog competition and the creative skills of the Craftsmen were traded for the gambling instinct. Moving along the edges of the developing economic frontier like vandals invading new territory, the Entrepreneurs took the risks and played the odds in order to accumulate massive fortunes and wield monopolistic power. Spiritually their devil-may-care attitude made them gods unto themselves. When the aged Andrew Carnegie tried to meet and make amends with Henry Clay Frick, a partner whom he had wronged, Frick rejected his offer with the curse, "Tell Mr. Carnegie that I'll meet him in hell."

† After the industrial frontier began to close around giant corporations, the ethic of work shifted once again. The *Career Ethic* personified by William Whyte's *Organization Man* and Maccoby's *Gamesman* took over where the entrepreneur left off. Now the motive for work became success in the system more than the accumulation of wealth. Process took priority over product, conformity replaced courage, and cooperation superseded competition. According to Maccoby, *gamesmen* who relished playing the system took over from the *jungle fighters* who lived and died by the bottom line. James McGregor Burns adds understanding to this changing work ethic when he identifies the hero of this era as the *transactional leader*, who masters the organizational process, rather than the *transformational leader*, who inspires others to follow by vision and charisma. [2] President Lyndon Johnson was one of those transactional heroes. He loved the in-workings of government, learned to sniff out the center of power, mastered the art of compromise, and relished making

the move as much as winning the game. One successful bureau-crat summed up the character of the *careerist* this way, "If you want to succeed in the system, keep your head down and your mouth shut." Spiritually, this kind of organization man is hard to fault because he conforms to the system, sins only in spirit, and offends no one, not even the devil. Of his kind, C.S. Lewis has Screwtape scoff about "their very smallness and flabbiness."[3] Even Satan would prefer the *robber baron* to the *organization man*.

† Today, we are living with yet another change in the work ethic that is shaping our national character. *The Self-fulfillment Ethic* is upon us. Rising out of the Me Generation of the 1970s and building upon the demands for individual rights, the Self-fulfillment Ethic makes the value of work secondary to the desire for personal satisfaction. Surveys show that vestiges of the Puritan Ethic are still with us in what is called a "giving/getting contract."[4] The person is willing to "give" work to "get" self-fulfillment. The balance, however, is tipped toward getting, not giving. The worker's priority demand is for a caring climate, job satisfaction, guaranteed security, and of course, the opportunity for self-realization. Entitlement or the belief that "You owe it to me" is the motive and equality is the standard that drives the Self-fulfillment Ethic. Young managers who were interviewed in a Bell System study epitomized the Self-fulfill-ment Ethic: "They don't want to lead, they don't want to fol-low. They want interesting work and satisfying emotional rela-tionships, characterized by 'kindness,' 'sympathy,' 'understand-ing' and 'generosity.' "[5]

Spiritually, those following the Self-fulfillment Ethic are getters more than givers. If they enter into a giving/getting contract for work, their persistent question is, "What's in it for me?" Their question, however, only leads to another. As the authors of the Bell System study put it, "With all our respect to the virtues of human warmth and kindness, who is going to run our corporations and make the tough decisions in the future?"

† While the Self-fulfillment Ethic may dominate the view of work among the younger generation, it is already being extended into new extremes of self-interest. The *Leisure Ethic* is one of those extremes. Leisure, by definition, is discretionary time over which we have control to use as we choose. As we have gained technical efficiency in the production of goods, our leisure time has markedly increased, especially among blue-collar workers. At the same time, white-collar workers such as executive officers are putting in sixty- and seventy-hour work weeks. The trend is clear. In times past, we had the leisure classes and the working masses. Today, the roles are reversed. We have the working classes and the leisure masses.

Good or bad, leisure has become the end for which we work. Daily work is valued not for its own sake, but as the necessary eight-hour path which takes us into leisurely evenings. Likewise, weekly work is done with an eye fixed toward a long weekend of leisure. Not unexpectedly, then, the working years are undertaken with early retirement in mind. In fact, the Leisure Ethic is upsetting the statistics of work. Early retirement is the fastest-growing phenomenon in our national labor force. In what appears to be a complete contradiction in the drive to make work a means for self-fulfillment, early retirement puts the premium upon leisure, not work, as the earthly ultimate in self-realization. Of course, not all early retirements are voluntary and not all are driven by self-interest. Some persons retire early to open another chapter of creativity and service in their lives. But when leisure is sought as an end in itself, it becomes the idolatrous substitute for work as a savior.

So we have seen that self-interest carries the seeds of its own destruction, whether in work or in leisure. Under the terms of the giving/getting contract, the reality of "giving" hard work without "getting" self-fulfillment is producing a career-weary people.[6] Early retirees who crowd our southern and southwestern states are still seeking self-fulfillment. Feeling as if they "paid their dues" in church and community service during their working years, they seek freedom from social and spiritual commitments that do not serve their leisure. Alas, they soon become leisure-weary. As one wealthy early retiree told me, "After six weeks of bowling, boats, and baseball, I went nuts." Too late, they learn that leisure is no more fulfilling than work when either is motivated by self-interest.

THE ETHIC OF A NEW AGE

Because Christians have failed to compose and communicate a biblical ethic of work, the false prophets of the New Age Movement have rushed into the vacuum created by the workers' search for meaning. Adopting a romantic view of work and neglecting its realities, New Agers extol daily work as an exciting and wonderful way for discovering the meaning of life. All of the New Age philosophy comes into play with the vision of re-creating ourselves and rediscovering our jobs. Meditative reflection raises consciousness to help us envision our full human potential on the job. Techniques of self-discipline and relational interaction guide us to reach the lofty, spiritualized state of a godlike nature.

The New Age approach to work should make us shudder. Its techniques are so close to the spiritual disciplines of Christianity that many innocent believers will be enraptured by its ideas. But its promises are patently false. Even though the New Age movement claims to be transcendental, it denies the supernatural and sovereign nature of a personal God. Instead, it assumes that a person can rise through semispiritual exercises to higher and higher levels of consciousness and ultimately arrive at self-fulfillment in a godlike nature. The movement twists the incarnational concept of "Christ in us" into the claim that each of us can be a god or Christ. Naturally, then, we have no need for a Redeemer.

Grim realities are also left behind, including the curse of sin which infects our human nature—spirit, body, mind, and soul—and contaminates our social order with injustice. The New Age attitude toward all of life, including work, is best voiced by Shirley Maclaine in her book, *Dancing in the Light*, when she tells an underachieving friend, "You are unlimited. You just don't realize it."[8]

What has gone wrong? By tracing the evolution of the work ethic in American history on the following chart, we see how far we have come from our biblical roots.

† Our work ethic has been separated from God. While the Puritan Ethic has been criticized for its rigidity, at least it had ties to the will of God. Once those ties were cut, workers began the long journey that has brought us to the New Age philosophy which claims, "We too can be gods." Idolatry is the end of our search for the meaning of work when we forsake God, rely upon ourselves, and still hold to the hope for self-fulfillment. The New Age Ethic is a bubble about to burst.

† Our work ethic has become increasingly self-centered. Again, if we use the Puritan Ethic as our base, the trend from communal responsibility to self-interest sounds an alarm. To see our daily work as a contribution to the physical, social, and moral quality of life in our community is the genius of American democracy. Not even the rise of the Entrepreneurial Ethic with its monopolistic capitalism could destroy the sense of communal responsibility. However greedy they may have been, the Vanderbilts, Morgans, Carnegies, and Rockefellers created charitable foundations which still represent their founders' commitment to the good of the community. Nor can we forget that during the tumultuous days of the Robber Barons, the long commitment of Americans to their community was formalized in non governmental human service agencies such as United Way, YMCA, YWCA, and Red Cross. Volunteerism for community service has its roots in the Puritan Work Ethic and, deeper yet,

OUR EVOLVING WORK ETHIC

ETHIC	MORAL	HERO	ADAGE
Puritan Ethic	Colonial Farmer	John Winthrop	"Do all for the glory of God."
Craftsman Ethic	Individual Tradesman	Benjamin Franklin	"God helps those who help themselves."
Entrepreneurial Ethic	Individual Giant	Andrew Carnegie	"It is the purest of wealth that invigorates life."
Career Ethic	Organizational Man	Oliver North	"If you want to succeed, keep your head down and your mouth shut."
Self-fulfillment Ethic	Executive Yuppie	Donald Trump	"What's in it for me?"
Leisure Ethic	Early Retiree	Bjorn Borg	"I've paid my dues."
New Age Ethic	Visionary Optimist	John Naisbitt	"You can be a god."

in the biblical meaning of the moral community whose members give themselves away to help others.

While government intrusion into public welfare has not been able to destroy those roots, the Leisure Ethic or the New Age Ethic can twist them into idolatrous ends. Christians should represent a counterculture to self-interest, in commitment to their communities and to voluntarily serving others. A Christian spirit of self-sacrifice will stand out in sharp relief against the rising self-interest in the contemporary culture.

† Our work ethic is becoming increasingly self-glorifying. According to the Westminster Shorter Catechism, "The chief end of man is to glorify God and enjoy Him forever." Sad to say, our revolving work ethic has strayed far from that confession. At least the Puritans believed in working hard for the glory of God. Self-glory began to rise immediately when the Craftsman Ethic shifted the goal of work to personal pride in the product. From there it was only a few steps into the *pride* of wealth, the *lust* for success, and the *demand* for self-fulfillment. Today, the person who follows the call of God in his or her work is judged as mildly fanatic or slightly mad. Sometimes, Christians are the severest critics. When I followed God's call from the Christian university to the seminary presidency, nonbelievers commended me while believers scratched their heads and asked, "Why leave the security of the university for the uncertainty of a new position?" It is one thing to profess our desire to glorify God; it is quite another thing to demonstrate it in our career decisions, especially our daily work.

TOWARD A BIBLICAL ETHIC

Our need for a biblical ethic to guide us in our daily work is urgent. As a starting point, we can draw the contrast between the secular and biblical ethic. A biblical ethic views work as a natural, creative gift of God, but that gift, as with all creation, has been spoiled by our sin. Therefore, our work needs to be redeemed by the call of God, for the good of the community and for the glory of God. Such a realistic and promising view cannot be separated from the momentous events of divine and human history—God's Creation, our Fall, and Christ's Redemption.

† The doctrine of Creation informs us that *work is a gift of God inseparable from our spiritual nature*. In the very first verse of Holy Scripture, we are introduced to God at work, "In the beginning, God created the heavens and the earth" (Genesis 1:1). The word *creation* is synonymous with the word *work* in the original Hebrew. Work, then, cannot be a curse or it would contradict the holiness of God. At the same time, work cannot be a savior or it would be disconnected from the creative purpose of God. Rather, God's work is spiritual—reflective of His holy character and representative of His divine purpose.

† Creation unveils another momentous truth that underlies the biblical theology of work. Because we are created in the image of God, *work is natural to our human existence and essential to our spiritual development*. Even in the Garden of Eden, God gave Adam and Eve work to do. In the first job description ever spoken or written, God gave His created human beings three work assignments. The first responsibility was *reproduction*, "Be fruitful and multiply"; the second was *production*, "Fill the earth and subdue it"; and the third was *supervision*, "Have dominion over the fish of the sea, over the birds of the air and over every living thing that moves on the earth" (Genesis 1:28).

God expected a lot from His creation. Yet, true to His character and consistent with the form of a good job description, he backed up Adam's responsibility for work with the rewards of His promise: "See, I have given you every herb that yields seed which is on the face of all the earth, and every tree whose fruit yields seed; to you it shall be for food" (Genesis 1:29).

OUR BIBLICAL ETHIC:
PARTNERS IN CREATION

In the second Genesis account of Creation, God upgraded His expectations and rewards for Adam's work. The Garden, originally a wilderness to be "tamed," was now a workplace for the more sophisticated task of "tending" (Genesis 2:15). Still another upgrade on the meaning of work awaited Adam. God recognized the loneliness of the task to which He called Adam, so He promised him a helper. With the creation of Eve, God established the relational meaning of human work.

God then honored the intellectual capacity of Adam by bringing all living creatures before him and inviting him to classify them and name them as evidence of his dominion over them (Genesis 2:19). In this task, we see the image of God in Adam and Eve demonstrated by the work of observing, wondering, reflecting, discerning, remembering, and communicating— abilities which are reserved for God and His humanity.

Adam and Eve's job description was not yet complete. God had given them physical, relational, and intellectual work assignments. Now He drew these all together in the spiritual promise of eternal life, but with a condition. They were not to eat fruit from the Tree of the Knowledge of Good and Evil. If they did, they would die (Genesis 2:17). The meaning of our work, therefore, has its limits. With the freedom of choice, the power of intellect, and the drive for self-realization which God has entrusted to us, we cannot tromp in the territory of His sovereignty by refusing to obey Him and pretending to be gods in our own right. Work which is separated from God, driven by self-interest, and finished in self-glory is condemned from the very beginning. For us, the spirituality of work must be confirmed as inseparable from God, motivated by His will, and done for His glory. In the doctrine of Creation, our daily work is dignified as a task with rewards that are inseparable from the image of God in us. No higher honor can come to our humanity than to exercise the privilege of being partners with God in the routine of our daily work.

† We cannot stop here. After the Creation came the Fall. The doctrine of the Fall leaves no doubt but that *our work is corrupted by our sin*. Work became one of the innocent victims of Adam and Eve's sin and no longer would be an unmixed joy. Instead, God passed the sentence for our sin on to the nature of our work: "Cursed is the ground for your sake; in toil you shall eat of it all the days of your life" (Genesis 3:17).

No longer would nature be a partner with human work. God said, "In the sweat of your face you shall eat bread" (Genesis 3:19). Despite all that we might say about the spirituality of work, we cannot deny that it is hard. I have a friend who conscientiously prepares himself for his daily work with a quiet time of prayer, meditation on Scripture, and a plan for priority tasks. Yet, he confesses so honestly, "When I hit the office door, all hell breaks loose." We all know what he means. In my case, a "personal/confidential" letter in the mail ruins my day, a grumpy colleague spoils my disposition, and continual interruptions upset my priorities. Hardly a day goes by but that I have to force myself to do some routine work, resent the lack of efficiency someplace in the institution, or wonder if God has misplaced me.

Of course, our evolving work ethic promises just the opposite. Advocates of the Self-fulfillment Ethic demand a work environment that is guaranteed to be compatible, cozy, and cuddly. If work is hard, they want relief; if work is routine, they want excitement; if work is restrictive, they want freedom; if work is lonely, they want company. The truth is that all work has its moments of being hard, routine, restrictive, and lonely. Instant gratification is a demand of the Self-fulfillment Ethic that work itself cannot fulfill. The curse of the ground and the sweat of the brow remain with us.

Christians should entertain no illusions about work. Until all creation is redeemed, we must learn to work diligently, patiently, and faithfully on long-term tasks for which the rewards are often deferred. As a seminary president whose desk could feature Harry Truman's sign, "The buck stops here," I often mutter to myself, "If only someone would say 'Thank you.'" In those moments, I need to make sure that I am still trying to do what is right for the good of the institution and in God's holy will. With that assurance, I regain my perspective and find peace, if not always joy, in my daily work.

† But there is hope. The doctrine of redemption informs us that *work is a resource to be redeemed.* Of course, work is not sinful in itself. As with all the gifts of God which were given to us in Creation, work is a victim of human sin. Only a sinner can make work itself a curse which becomes an excuse for sin, or a savior which becomes an idol flaunting God. Conversely, only a Christian can make work a means of grace through which the gift of God flows. Paul, for instance, used his skills at tentmaking as the way to earn not only his living, but also to gain his credibility when he sought to evangelize cities on his missionary journeys.

One of the most powerful portraits that shows the connection between work and spirituality is a painting by Holman Hunt which hangs in the city gallery in Manchester, England. Jesus is depicted at work with His tools, shaping the pieces of wood on the carpenter's bench. Fading light from the window picks up the silhouette of His work and casts it as a shadow against the wall. At the same time, Jesus stretches and raises both hands above His head. The pieces of wood become a cross in those shadows and Jesus becomes the crucified victim. In this awesome art, we see not only a prophetic picture of Jesus' death, but also an unforgettable symbol of the connection between His daily work and His spiritual mission.

Through Christ's redemption our daily work is restored to its spiritual meaning in the Creation story. The nature of work is redeemed as a gift of God and, once redeemed, our daily work becomes a means of grace. The end of our work is an offering given for the glory of God.

   ✝   When we see our daily work as a means of grace, the highest truth comes home to us: When accepted as a gift of God, done under the call of God, and finished to the glory of God, *our daily work involves us as partners with God in continuing creation.* Again, the distinction between the work of animalkind and humankind becomes clear. Only human beings created in the image of God can do creative work which is to:

> envision a task to be done,
> imagine a solution to a problem,
> evaluate the quality of results,
> communicate what has been learned to the
> coming generation,
> feel satisfied with the connection to a larger
> purpose such as the good of the community
> and the will of God.

Of course, these criteria apply to all the work of human beings, Christian or not. Our daily work is intended to be natural, purposeful, and creative. But when sin undermines these intentions, our daily work becomes either a curse or a savior. What was intended to be a creative relationship with God has been broken. This brokenness can be redeemed only by grace. Once redeemed, however, our daily work becomes the means through which we rediscover the Creation Ethic, which defines work according to biblical principles, in partnership with God and toward the spiritual end of His declaration, "It is very good."

†

SPIRITUAL REFLECTIONS ON OUR BIBLICAL ETHIC

As each one has received a gift, minister it to one another, as good stewards of the manifold grace of God.

1 Peter 4:10

A PROVOCATIVE QUESTION

How do you think people perceive you in your daily work? Would you be considered a craftsman, a jungle fighter, a company man, or a gamesman? How about your work ethic? Are you primarily motivated by good pay, creative opportunity, compatible people, self-fulfillment, leisure time, early retirement, or some other incentive? How does being a Christian make a difference?

A PRACTICAL EXERCISE

Our attitude toward work is strongly influenced by our upbringing. What attitude toward work did your parents communicate to you? Did their model match their words? Did they impress you with mottoes such as, "Hard work never hurt anyone" or "Any job worth doing is worth doing well"? What connection did your parents make between work and spirituality?

A PERSONAL PRAYER

Lord, deliver me from the subtle and secular influence that steals the spiritual meaning from my daily work. Never let me forget that I am Your partner in creation every day. Amen

FOUR

FIRST PRINCIPLE: WORK IS PRAYERFUL

*W*here do you want to go?"
"I don't know."
"Then, any direction will do."
—Alice and the Mad Hatter

Clump, clump, clump . . . pat, pat, pat. We were awakened by the hurried sound of big feet and the catch-up sound of little feet over our heads. More footsteps followed like an audio version of Goldilocks—Daddy Bear, Mamma Bear, and three Baby Bears. We laughed as we envisioned the drama unfolding upstairs. With each passing minute, the tempo of the footsteps picked up until big feet stomped and little feet ran. Then, with the slam of a door and the whir of an auto engine, the house fell silent. "Whew," my wife said to me, "they made it again."

We had just listened to the sounds of our son's family getting ready for work and school. To accommodate us when we visit him, he had built a brand-new parents' room in his basement. Always before, we had stayed in a second-floor bedroom and had missed the early morning drama. Both he and his wife work, two older children are in grade school, and the youngest is in preschool. Every morning, then, is a race against time and a test of family organization. Until we heard the sounds above, we had not realized how fast the modern family has to move under pressure.

Does the story sound familiar? My guess is that each of us identifies with the sound and sometimes the fury of our families getting ready for work and school. Noticeably missing in the fast-moving drama is the interlude of quiet time for prayer in preparation for the work of the day. Of course, we heard all feet stop for a brief blessing at breakfast, but then the anxious tapping began again during hurried bites and took on the sound of a stampede from the table to the bathroom and out the door.

PRAYER AS PREPARATION FOR OUR WORK

Modern life militates against prayer as preparation for our daily work. Now that our household is an empty nest, I find time for solitude and spiritual reflection in the morning. When our four children were home, however, my morning model for the children was "prayer on the run." Sometime during the day they might see me alone with my Bible, and we finally settled on Sunday night as the time reserved for family prayer. During the week, our regular prayer time fell during the pre-meal moments when we tried to gather the family at our round table for dinner.

Prayer on the run is no substitute for the "brooding time" which preceded God's creative work in the Genesis story. When I was in the busy work cycle with my family, I remember the comfort I received from the title of Malcolm Boyd's book, *Are You Running with Me, Jesus?* The title implies the speed of our spiritual activism which requires Jesus to run and catch up. Of course, this is nothing more than a show of spiritual arrogance. Yet, I bought into the idea because I needed to justify my lack of "brooding time" alone with God. I remember rationalizing my prayerlessness by contending that "prayer *on* the run" for a Christian college president doing the Lord's work was just as good as "prayer *before* the run." Also, I hid behind the weak excuse that the "quality of prayer" was more important than the "quantity of prayer." Neither excuse holds water. I still pray on the run, but those petitions are usually spotty and self-serving. If only I had followed God's example of "brooding time" long ago, my daily work would have been more effective and my spiritual growth would have been greater.

The monastic fathers disciplined their daily lives according to the Latin motto *laborare est orare*, or "to work is to pray." After early hours of meditation, they went to a full day of menial labor and then returned to evening prayers before retiring for the night. Spiritually, however, their prayers were primary. They worked only for sustenance; true spirituality came through the discipline of their devotions. During the hours when they worked, they continued in the attitude of prayerful discipline.

Prayer in the Creation Ethic is different. According to Genesis 1:2, the Spirit "brooded" over the dark waters and the empty earth. Because brooding is a form of prayer, the motto of the monks, *laborare est orare*, might well be applied to the Creation Ethic. But there is an essential difference. For the monastic fathers, prayer had spiritual priority over work; for the Spirit of God in Creation, prayerful planning served as preparation for effective work. Neither praying nor doing had priority. Each had spiritual value of its own. Let's look at some of the ways that prayer prepares us for our daily work.

PRAYER AS PERSPECTIVE FOR OUR WORK

Prayer prepares us for our daily work by giving us perspective. Daily labor has a way of engaging the mind and spirit so thoroughly that we can become obsessed with our tasks. The results can be detrimental to our person as well as to our work. For instance, our work suffers from the "law of diminishing returns" because details overwhelm us. Also, our sense of personal worth suffers because our worth is too closely tied to our work.

In his book *Modern Madness: The Emotional Fallout of Success,* Douglas LaBier notes an increasing tendency for people to bind together their personal identity with their professional career. "Indeed," he writes, "they are almost equivalent."[1] But people who identify too closely with their work lose their objectivity and see every problem on the job as either a threat or an enhancement of their self-image. In severe cases, the ensuing stress may lead to psychological anxiety, physical illness, or social conflicts.

In a *Psychology Today* article entitled, "Is Your Job Driving You Crazy?" Ronni Sandroff lists some of the risks of identifying too closely with our jobs and taking ourselves too seriously.[2] In one way or another, every one of us can find ourselves on the list.

> Clergy: Supreme Self-Denial—developing a distorted view of self-sacrifice which causes us to ignore our own needs and fail with others.

> Police Officer: Rambo Complex—being unable to admit fears and vulnerabilities.

> Teachers: Submissive Savant—exaggerating their own powerlessness and fear of confronting authority.

> Lawyers: Verdict Vertigo—crumbling under the weight of responsibility and fear of making a mistake.

> Dentists: Psychic Cavities—focusing upon technical skills, but having trouble with people, particularly their own families.

Government Workers: Uncle Sam Syndrome—developing lethargic, automaton behavior.

Computer Programmers: Techno-Personality—finding human beings frustrating because they're too hard too fix.

Performers: Hamlet's Doubt—after gaining public acclaim, they still have the empty feeling, "Is this all?"

Politicians: Image Attachment—believing their own propaganda and the images they project to the public.

Physicians: M.D.-eity Syndrome—failing in battle against pain, disease and death, their idealism suffers.

Therapists: Pernicious Ph.D.-eity—running the risk of becoming grandiose as they have trouble dropping their interpretative and restrained professional role.

Air Traffic Controllers: Quick Fixers—expressing discomfort with the ambiguities of human situations.

Stock Brokers: Money Mania—falling into the habit of spending money as the way of expressing themselves.

Each of us can add to the list. When we lose the "white space" between our identity and our work, we become miserable and boring persons whom others want to avoid. When we take ourselves too seriously and lose our identity in our work, we have no room to change, stretch, grow, or flex, either on the job or as persons.

"Brooding time" in prayer keeps us from taking ourselves too seriously. When we pray, we step back from our daily work and into the setting where we are all alone with God—very small in His presence, but very significant as eternal and total beings in comparison with the temporary and partial nature of our jobs. At one and the same time, we see our work as infinitely meaningful and patently absurd. To realize that we are cocreators with God gives our daily work infinite meaning; to realize how small a difference our work will make in the history of the world lets us laugh at ourselves. Senator Sam Ervin, Chairman of the Senate Committee investigating the Watergate scandal, was asked if he was ready for such a crucial and controversial role. Ervin answered, "I've been preparing all of my life for this moment." With humility and humor, then, he brought an objectivity to his chairmanship that kept him from grandstanding and left everyone with the impression that he was wise and fair with all parties. As we know, Sam Ervin was a man who knew the value of "brooding time" in prayer.

Each day, then, we need to prepare for work with prayer. Such a discipline is not only spiritually sound, but is also mentally necessary. Experts in time management recommend daily "brooding" as preparation for effective work. A simple technique of listing tasks to be done and then sorting them out according to their priorities: urgent and essential

timely and important

long-range and optional

restores perspective to our work and multiplies our efficiency. Even when our work plan is upset by interruptions, we retain our perspective. Henri Nouwen, the professor-priest, tells of resenting students who interrupted his scholarly writing until one day he realized that the students were the reason for his calling to teaching. From that perspective he said, "Interruptions are my business."[3]

In one way or another, each of us needs to set a schedule of "brooding time" in preparation for our daily work. My pattern involves solitary time both morning and night. Late every night, I jog along the nearly abandoned streets in our village. I am so regular on the run that students of the seminary have nicknamed me "The Midnight Strider." They know that I want to be alone; I need the time to regain my perspective. No Walkman fills my ears with the sound of music or teaching tapes. The built-in recorder of my brain frees my mind from the clutter of the day and prepares me for the work load of tomorrow. The first ten minutes or so is "sorting time." I store extraneous events of the day in the memory bank of "Things to Forget," including failures, criticisms, and hurts which are not worth either a response or a continuing memory. One of the most significant phrases that I recall speaking to myself after weighing a personal grievance is, "It's not worth my time or energy. I have more important things to do."

Eighteen to twenty minutes into my jogging I experience the "runner's high." Whether it is physiological or psychological, it translates into a spiritual experience for me. After reaching that high, I have not only put my daily work back into the perspective of my spiritual calling, but have had unforgettable moments of "creative breakthroughs" with solutions to problems, outlines for speeches, and imaginative thoughts for long-range planning. Most important of all, at least for me, my anxiety about the future is lifted and I return home to sleep with the "sweet amen of peace."

In those memorable moments, I feel a kinship with the Spirit of God who "brooded" over the dark waters and empty earth before proceeding with His creative work. Chaos, darkness, and emptiness characterize my world as well. Without "brooding time" and prayer with God alone, the world is too much for me. But if I step back and gain the perspective of prayer, I see the creative potential in my work for order to come from chaos, light from darkness, and fullness from emptiness.

PRAYER AS PLANNING FOR OUR WORK

With the perspective of brooding prayer, the Spirit of God turned from an architect to an engineer. An architect is a designer who works from an artist's perspective; an engineer is a detailer who works with a technician's precision. Most people are one or the other, either a designer or a detailer. The most creative person I have known, however, combined the two. Ed Wells is best known as the ingenious man who engineered the breakthroughs in succeeding generations of Boeing Aircraft. He is a stickler for details and rigidly obedient to the laws of physics and aerodynamics. Ed brings that same discipline to his avocational love of oil painting. Yet, his art is as creative as his aircraft. In describing his work, he speaks about the precision of planning the design, mixing the colors, and laying out the painting. But once his brush touches the canvas he is set free. Form, line, and color come together in an artistic creation that is very good and very valuable. It all begins with the detailed planning of brooding time.

Between the lines of the Genesis story, we can imagine the mind of the Spirit at work with thoughts of creating *order* out of chaos, turning darkness to *light*, and changing emptiness to *fullness*.

Order is created by a grand ecological design in which everything is connected with everything else and all is centered in God; *light* is the generating force for living and growing beings; and *fullness* is the totality of minerals, vegetables, and animal life crowned by human beings created in the "image of God."

Our work will take on similar designs and dimensions in creative thought during our brooding times when the Spirit moves upon our minds and hearts as He did over the dark waters of the unformed earth. Each morning I lay out my daily work before God and ask that He do His brooding once again so that my plans coincide with the "strategy of the Spirit." Failure to follow this spiritual discipline takes me into the "strategy of self" which might include plans to attack enemies, ploys for winning against competitors, or patterns of random action without a clear sense of direction.

No matter what the nature of our work, we need to plan in prayer. On a typical day we each face decisions which affect the quality of our work—tasks that are too big for us, people who are too difficult for us, and problems that are too complicated for us. For each of these, we need preventive prayer which gives us a sense of who we are and of where we are going. Planning each day through the discipline of prayer will keep us on track and carry us through the inevitable highs and lows of our daily work.

PRAYER AS ENERGY FOR OUR WORK

Another advantage comes from prayer as preparation for our daily work. Perspective gives us a "big picture" of the work to be done and planning breaks down major projects into manageable tasks. Together, then, perspective and planning bring our diverse energies into high-intensity focus. In the oft-quoted Scripture, we say "The effective, fervent prayer of a righteous man avails much" (James 5:16). This passage is more than a prooftext for the results of prayer. We may miss the point that *effective* and *fervent* are adjectives describing the nature of prayer. Without violence to the text, we might also describe the prayer that avails much as *focused* and *energized*. When we do, our understanding of the verse is assisted by the laws of physics. Whenever light or heat is focused with high intensity, the results can be a laser beam that has power to pierce steel or a nuclear bomb that can obliterate cities. Wind that is focused has similar energy. When a low-pressure frontal system penetrates a high-pressure area, the power of the wind at the point of penetration has tornado force.

Pinpoint prayer has the same power. When we prepare for our daily work through the discipline of prayer, all of our energies are focused upon the task and energized by the power of concentration. Eastern gurus, New Age cultists, and motivational therapists have tried to capitalize on this principle of prayer through such techniques as meditation, visioning, and centering. Certainly they have succeeded from the human standpoint, because the principle is psychological as well as spiritual. Yet they are limited to the natural dimensions of the practice. Only prayer which focuses body, mind, and soul on God, and submits to His will, has the energy of divine and human power which can move mountains and make miracles.

When we fail to pray, however, our perspective for work narrows. Our plans for work give way to chaos and our energy for work is drained. We need to brood over our daily tasks with focused and energized prayer if we want our work to be creative.

Experience has taught me that I can miss my nightly jogging for three days before I notice personal fatigue, muscular regression, and loss of body tone. The discipline of prayer, however, does not afford me the sáme luxury, for there is a direct and immediate effect between my life of prayer and my life of work. If I miss my solitude in prayer, either in the morning or evening, my outlook changes, my energy lags, and my work suffers.

None of us can afford to begin our daily work without brooding time in prayer. The Creation story tells us why. Without this brooding time in the presence of God to know the mind of the Spirit and the Word of Christ, our daily work will be like the heavens and the earth in the beginning—dark, empty, and chaotic.

SPIRITUAL REFLECTIONS ON OUR WORK AND PRAYER

> For we are His workmanship, created in Christ Jesus for good works, which God prepared beforehand that we should walk in them.
>
> Ephesians 2:10

A PROVOCATIVE QUESTION

Do you have daily "brooding time" when you practice the discipline of prayer? What time is best for you? What disciplines do you practice? Have you found a direct connection between the regularity of your "brooding time," the quality of your work, and the evidence of your spiritual growth?

A PRACTICAL EXERCISE

Make a prayer list which identifies the critical aspects of your daily work. Include your relationships, your work environment, and the tasks you must do. Then, pray for a new attitude, new energy, and new results in your daily work.

A PERSONAL PRAYER

Father, forgive me for substituting "busy work" for "brooding time" as the way to do Your will. Amen

FIVE

SECOND PRINCIPLE: WORK IS VOCATIONAL

I think most of us are looking for a calling, not a job. Most of us, like the assembly-line worker, have jobs that are too small for our spirits."[3]

—Studs Terkel

A thousand images race through our minds when we read, "In the beginning God created the heavens and the earth." We may envision the voice of God speaking the world into existence out of nothing; the finger of God pointing to the place in the universe where heaven and earth are to be; or the feet of God stepping out on space so that He can survey His creation. Whatever image comes to mind, one common truth holds all the images together: God is introduced to us as *God at work!*

If work is natural to the character and function of God, it must be inherently good. Of course, the Fall of Adam and Eve in the Garden put the taint of sin upon work, just as it did upon all other aspects of God's creation. Still, not even sin could destroy God's intention for human work. Because work is so natural to God's character, we must believe that part of Christ's total plan in dying on the cross was to redeem our work. In other words, the biblical meaning of *vocation* is related to redemption. To be a Christian is to be in vocation—called of God for a special task consistent with our individual gifts, and woven into the rich and varied fabric which represents the unity of the body of Christ.

THE LANGUAGE OF VOCATION

Vocation is one of those strong words which needs to be recovered in our Christian vocabulary. Language so often betrays our loss of biblical truth and moral values. When the Roman Catholic Church separated the spiritual work of the sanctuary from the secular work of the marketplace, the biblical meaning of *vocation* fell on the spiritual side. Such a distortion of biblical truth had far-reaching implications for the church and society. The religious were called to spiritual vocations; all other people were punished for their sin by labor in the marketplace. The church, as the expression of spiritual vocation, stood with dictatorial dominance over government, education, and commerce. Its segregation of the sacred from the profane justified such evils as the divine right of kings and the feudal system of lords and peasant slaves.

No wonder Martin Luther worked to restore the biblical meaning of vocation as part and parcel of the Reformation. For him, a corollary of the "priesthood of believers," which broke the barriers between clergy and laity, was the "vocation of all believers," which removed the wall between spiritual and secular work. According to Luther, all believers are called of God, according to their gifts, to a vocation which is spiritual. I remember so well my struggle with a vocational choice between higher education and pastoral ministry. Luther rescued me with the good words, "It is more spiritual for a cobbler to use good leather and a strong stitch than it is to pass out tracts." From then on I could go either way, as God might call.

SECOND PRINCIPLE:
WORK IS VOCATIONAL

Despite Luther's efforts, the biblical word *vocation* has continued to be perverted and usurped by secular language. The perversion is to use the word strictly in the skill and training context. "Vocational" schools and "vocational" training apply to trade schools. Nothing is wrong with specialized training and manual skills. But to call this kind of education "vocational" robs the concept of its basis in God's calling and narrows the term to mean an educational experience with little or no emphasis upon foundational learning in the liberal arts from which we get our intellectual and moral heritage.

At the present time, higher education is caught in a cycle of "careerism"—a secular substitute for biblical vocation. Students are choosing major fields of study that lead directly to profitable careers in business, computer science, and communications. Left behind are the traditional majors in the liberal arts, such as humanities, natural science, social science, philosophy, and religion.

Of course, careerism has long been with us. Whether for students at Harvard in the seventeenth century opting for the professions of medicine, law, and ministry, or for students in Christian colleges during this century migrating toward teaching, nursing, and business, professional careers have always been attractive. The difference today is that *self-interest without moral responsibility* seems to dictate the choice. Since 1966, the American Council on Education has surveyed incoming college freshmen each year to ascertain their educational aspirations. In the first surveys of the late 1960s, approximately seventy percent of the freshmen aspired to develop a philosophy of life as a primary outcome of their education. Less than forty percent saw college as an opportunity to become well-off financially. Twenty years later in the late 1980s, the statistics were reversed. Seventy percent of the freshmen saw college as a step toward financial success and less than forty percent aspired primarily to develop a philosophy of life. Not surprisingly, the majority of students today are choosing careers offering the promise of financial return. Self-interest also causes them to take safe courses, avoid moral questions, and remain provincial in their outlook. At least in its current meaning, *careerism* is the antithesis of *vocation*.

Other terms which have replaced vocation are *job, occupation,* and *business.* Again, there is nothing wrong with these terms in their specialized meaning. They are not, however, synonyms for vocation. For one thing, the terms are too small. The word *job* captures only a small segment of a person. Referring almost exclusively to a task to be done, it lacks the spiritual, moral, personal, and communal breadth and depth of such a rich biblical word as *vocation.* Much is written and said about the depersonalization of technical systems in our modern world. However, much of this depersonalization begins with definitions. The word *job* implies no divine calling, neglects the totality of human personality, ignores the interpersonal nature of human work, draws no lines of moral obligation to the larger community, and promises no frontiers for growth. A job can be stripped down to nothing more than an impersonal, amoral, or antisocial task by which we exchange production for pay. No wonder so many of our college graduates who aspired as college freshmen to become well-off financially are shuttling from career to career without the satisfaction which they hoped salary, status, success, and security would bring. No wonder that so many of them are pursuing the impossible—trying to combine commitment with the self-interest in a giving/getting contract.

A BIBLICAL MEANING OF VOCATION

What then is the biblical meaning of *vocation?* The meaning rises out of the premise that work is inherent in God's spiritual nature and, therefore, also essential to our spirituality. As J. H. Oldham notes in his book *Work in Modern Society,* "Work is inherent in

God's purpose of man and an essential experience of man's nature as created in the image of God, the Creator."[1] Such an affirmation sets the stage for understanding the biblical meaning of vocation as relational and redemptive.

Our fundamental premise is that *biblical vocation is relational*. While work is essential to human nature, it is only part of our nature. In the Garden of Eden, Adam and Eve enjoyed a compatible relationship with God, nature, and each other. Although those relationships were spiritual, they were sustained by practical functions. Worship nurtured Adam and Eve's relationship with God; work maintained their relationship with nature; and wedlock was the lifeline for their love.

Vocation means being called of God to each of those interlocking relationships. To isolate worship from work, work from wedlock, or wedlock from worship is to lose the wholeness which is God's first vocational call upon our lives. To violate one of those relationships is even more destructive. Without exception, sin is an intentional break in our relationship with God, nature, or each other. By eating the fruit in violation of God's command, Adam and Eve found themselves alienated from God. One of the most plaintive cries of human history is God's call in the Garden to Adam and Eve, "Where are you?"

Once they broke with God, Adam and Eve turned on each other and then were driven from the Garden into the wilds of antagonistic nature. In reality, *sin is a lost vocation*—denying the call of God, violating the sacred relationship of worship, work, or wedlock, and discovering that our spiritual alienation affects the whole of life.

Our corollary premise follows: *Biblical vocation is redemptive*. Ever since God called Adam and Eve in the Garden, He has beckoned every person in every generation back to his true vocation. In other words, the purpose of God's call is to redeem people and restore the relationships of worship, work, and wedlock which were severed by sin in the Fall. In both the Old and

New Testaments, we hear this call from God. When we do, we learn that biblical vocation has meaning in three progressive steps.

† God's first call is to faith. Immediately we see that the biblical meaning of vocation is far more than a call to a job; it is *a call to a commitment.* In the Old Testament, we see this meaning of vocation activated when God calls the Children of Israel to be His chosen people. By responding with faith in God and love for Him, the Israelites became the covenant people for whom the divine-human relationship was restored. Both individually and collectively, the Israelites became heirs of the promise which God had given to Abraham. More than that, as members of the covenant community, they received the revelation of the Law which served as the guide for their other relationships in life—work and wedlock as well as worship.

The Apostle Paul extended this same vocational calling to the Gentiles when he declared that they became "heirs with Israel, members of the body and partakers of the promise" because of faith in Jesus Christ (Ephesians 3:6). This is the new "testament" or "covenant" of our calling which is in effect today. We understand, then, why Paul went to urge the Ephesian Christians to "walk worthy of the vocation" by which they are called (Ephesians 4:1) and immediately proceeds to talk about their spiritual relationships as members of "one body, one Spirit, one hope, one Lord, one faith, one baptism, one God and Father of all" (vv. 4-5). Later, the Apostle goes on to talk about the specifics of our work. But first and foremost, our vocation is to answer God's gracious call to the faith which restores our relationship with Him and gives us the privilege of being the children of His new covenant in Christ.

† God's second call is to growth in our gifts. From among His people in the Old Testament, He called certain persons with particular gifts to be His prophets. This is our prototype for the *vocational call to a commission.* Prophets were sanctified or "set apart" for the special task of speaking the Word of God to a wayward people. John the Baptist and Jesus were the last in the line of the prophets, and each of them is introduced to us as men who were "sent" from God. "Set apart" and "sent" describe the process out of which prophets—a rare and select breed of spiritual people—were made. After Pentecost, however, the prophets' privilege became a possibility for all believers. Through the agency of the Holy Spirit, what has been called a "cosmos of callings" opened up to us. Each and every person who is alive in Christ has a *charisma* or gift through which he or she can contribute to the effective ministry of the body of Christ and grow to full potential as a person created in the image of God. Biblical vocation advances with God's call upon the distinctive gifts that He has given to us. Even if our gifts are in a nonreligious field, our vocational call is to acknowledge them, cultivate them, and use them for the glory of God. The witness of "prophets without portfolio" in secular professions is indispensable to God's redemptive purpose in the world.

† God's third call is to a task which is uniquely ours to do. After He has chosen us to be His covenant people and commissioned us for the growth of our gifts, God calls us to *vocational consecration* for a special task. In other words, our job is the point where our vocational call to faith and growth come together in special focus. Not that our job is spiritually inferior to our covenant or our commission. Just as our vocational relationships of worship, work, and wedlock cannot be isolated or violated, so our three vocational appointments are equally interlocked and interdependent. Although the idea is not popular now, the coherence of our vocational appointments helps us understand why Paul wrote:

> For he who was a slave when he was called by
> the Lord is the Lord's freedman; similarly, he
> who was a free man when he was called is

Christ's slave. You were bought at a price; do not become slaves of men. Brethren, each man, as responsible to God should remain in the situation God called him to (1 Corinthians 7:22-24, NIV).

Contrary to some opinions, Paul is not condoning slavery. Rather he is appraising the freedom that comes with the call of God. More important than our station in life or the job we hold is our relationship to God. Whether we are slave or free, servant or master, laborer or leader, the call of God puts us all on common ground vocationally. How else can we understand the joy of a janitor who whistles while he works or the testimony of a redeemed prisoner who spoke through steel bars, "They have my body in here, but not my soul. I am a free man"?

OUR TWO JOBS

Every person comes to two different jobs each day. One job is a special task to be done, requiring the application of hand and mind for full productivity. The other job takes in the larger working environment and includes the climate for work, the attitude of workers, and the margins for personal and professional growth. People who go only to the first job end up despising their work and devaluing themselves. Persons with a sense of vocation, however, go each day to two jobs. They will work for quality production at their specific task, but they will also work to change the working environment by their attitudes and find new avenues for personal and professional growth within the margins of their role. Once we discover those margins, however, Christians can be expected to break out into new dimensions of freedom and opportunity. Isn't that why Paul urged Christians who were slaves to take advantage of the opportunity for freedom? I suspect that he would have been brutal with a believer who forfeited freedom because of contentment as a slave.

What about people who cannot work? For those of us who are gainfully employed, it is easy to assume that everyone can work if they want to. We forget a welfare system that discourages ambition. Recently, I became an advocate for a divorced mother who is impoverished because she prefers to work as a secretary rather than subsist on welfare. By firsthand experience, I also became an advocate of "workfare." We must not forget those who want to work and can't. When Toyota opened a new auto plant just north of our home in Kentucky, 200,000 people applied for 1,200 jobs. None of us expect Christians to settle for unemployment when they can work. Yet, during those difficult times which can befall any of us, Christians do not lose their vocational calling. They know their call to faith as God's covenant people and they know their call to develop their gifts as God's commissioned people. While this sense of vocation has holding power during times of unemployment, it will not put bread on the table. Therefore, every Christian has an obligation to these members of the faith to employ them, to recommend them for work, to lobby for their welfare, and, if necessary, to sustain them as members of the community of faith so that each is served according to his needs (Acts 2:45).

Our biblical vocation, then, is a calling from God that begins with our salvation when we are chosen to enter the covenant of faith; it continues in our sanctification when we are commissioned to exercise our special gifts, and is finalized in our consecration to the specific task or situation which we call our daily work.

We cannot isolate or violate any of these appointments without sacrificing the essence of life, the fullness of life promised in Christ, and the spiritual potential of God's calling to vocation.

ANSWERING GOD'S CALL

At one time or another, each of us asks the question, "How do I know God's calling for my life?" College students, in particular, find this question nagging them as they try to match the will of God with the nearly unlimited options for careers. Whenever I counsel with these students, I cite the three "Rs" of vocational choice: reason, righteousness, and revelation.

† Reason is a direct tie-in with the creative process. Because we are created *Imago Dei*—in the image of God—we are endowed with the intellectual ability to think logically, plan critically, and act constructively. It should come as no surprise, therefore, to learn that God expects us to exercise our capability of reasoning in vocational decisions. Of course, the starting point in our search for guidance is the Word of God. A chapel speaker at a Christian college once told the students, "Ninety-eight percent of the answers to our vocational questions are in the Bible. If only we would read and reflect upon the Word of God." He may have overstated his case, but the fundamental truth is sound. We cannot spiritualize our vocational decisions or expect God to answer by splitting the skies, when we have not exercised fully the gift of sound thinking and common sense that He has given us. Late last night, for instance, panic filled the voice of a prospective student who called me to appeal for admission to seminary. He won an audience with me immediately with his enthusiastic plea, "God has called me to preach, I have been looking forward to attending Asbury all my life, my car is packed and it's in the driveway pointing toward Kentucky right now." Puzzled, I asked, "But why were you not admitted?" Slowly, the story unfolded. He had college grades below our probationary level, test scores too low to make up the difference, and a late application without adequate references. As gently as possible, I told him that he had studied too little, started too late, and expected too much. Eventually, we worked

out an optional plan which would let him be admitted later if he proved his ability, developed his discipline, and prepared himself for graduate study.

Serious reflection and inquiry are needed to draw realistic guidelines for vocational planning. Well-conceived and tested vocational instruments are available to help us delimit the fields which match our interest for working with things, numbers, or people. Of course, these are no substitutes for exploratory experiences in jobs or internships to enable us to sort out work that we love, tolerate, or despise. For me, a full summer as a hod carrier for a bricklayer, who finally let me lay up a crooked corner, convinced me that my talents and interests should be "laid" elsewhere. More often than not, the exercise of reason will be sufficient to identify our vocational gifts and focus our career options without asking God to do the screening and sorting for us.

† Righteousness parallels reason in the process of vocational choice. Of course, we know that we have no righteousness of our own. Only as we trust in Christ for our redemption, can we lay any claim to His righteousness. At the same time, we cannot rely upon reason alone as the basis for making our vocational choice. God's will must be our will. Therefore, when I counsel with students who are struggling with career decisions, I follow my question about the exercise of reason with the penetrating probe, "Does His Spirit witness with your spirit that you are a child of God?" Without an affirmative answer, we cannot go on. Unless our heart is clear before God, we are not open to the leading of His Spirit, wherever and whatever that may be. There is no substitute for that high moment when the student answers, "Yes, I'll go where He wants me to go and do what He wants me to do." A path of faith into a bright and expanding horizon opens before us when we sign a blank letter of trust and let God fill in the details.

† Revelation may appear to be a shortcut around reason

and righteousness—one that we want God to take when He calls us into vocation. But God doesn't work that way. He expects us to exercise fully our capacity for reason and follow the providential leading of His Spirit as we trust in His righteousness alone. But on rare occasions, our faithfulness to reason and righteousness still leaves us uncertain about the path we should take. Fleece after fleece may come up dry. Sometimes, in those moments, God wants us to take just a step at a time without our destination clearly in view.

My vocational walk with God, for instance, is filled with zigs and zags. At each turning point in my educational and professional career, I didn't foresee the implications of decisions I made when I changed majors, expanded fields, tested options, tried different positions, and hopscotched among institutions. But looking back, I bow in gratitude before the wisdom of God which gave providential direction to what would otherwise be labeled as a checkerboard career. More than once along my vocational path, I found myself without an answer after exhausting my reason and renewing my spiritual commitment. In those moments, I dared to beg God for a supernatural break in the natural order—a special revelation to show me the way. He has always answered, not by my preferred timing or style, but usually with a confirmation of direction which I should have seen but had chosen to ignore. In each case, God also accomplished His revelation with the words of eternal patience, "Trust Me."

LIVING WORTHY OF OUR VOCATION

Carlisle called *vocation* one of the "loveliest of words." Its nature is inherent in the character of God, its relationships embrace the vitality of life, and its appointments give full meaning to the dignity of human personality. *Vocation* is to be redeemed by the witness of Christians in their daily work just as Christ redeemed it in His work on the cross. The Apostle Paul grasped the importance of this witness for his day when he urged the Ephesians, "Walk worthy of the calling with which you were called" (Ephesians 4:1, NIV).

Our vocation is a sacred trust. Redeemed by the Lord, we go to our daily work with the calling of being His covenant people, exercising His spiritual gifts, and doing His holy will in productive labor, quality work, and community responsibility. To live worthy of our vocational calling is practical proof of our redeemed nature.

✝
SPIRITUAL REFLECTIONS ON OUR WORK AND CALLING

I, therefore, the prisoner of the Lord, be-
seech you to have a walk worthy of the
calling with which you were called.

Ephesians 4:1

A PROVOCATIVE QUESTION

How have you responded to God's threefold vocational call upon your life?

Have you answered to God's call into the covenant of faith?

Have you been "set apart" for a purpose which utilizes your natural talents?

Have you consecrated your daily work to God?

A PRACTICAL EXERCISE

Think forward into your vocational future. Where is God leading you vocationally? Is your long-term goal clear or is He leading you a step at a time?

A PERSONAL PRAYER

O Ever Faithful Christ, may I truly be worthy of my calling—to a personal faith, to an individual gift, and to a special task. Amen

---

SIX

THIRD PRINCIPLE: WORK IS RELATIONAL

*T*he university would be a great place to teach if it weren't for the students."
—A university professor

Creation is a relational act of God. When we read, "In the beginning, God created the heavens and the earth," we envision God the Father working alone to make a world and fashion His creation. But Creation was a cooperative act of the Trinity— God the Father, God the Son, and God the Holy Spirit. Initially, they may have worked as one in focused power to create the world out of nothing. Then they divided their labor according to the unique expression of the Godhead that they represent throughout divine revelation.

God the Father is the *executive* of the Trinity. He oversees the work and makes judgment on its quality. God the Holy Spirit is the *architect*, who performs the task of brooding over the dark void and chaotic world to plan its grand design. God the Son, then, works as the *engineer* of the Trinity. He speaks the word and "All things were made through Him, and without Him nothing was made that was made" (John 1:3).

Throughout the Creation story, throughout biblical revelation, and throughout human history, the Trinity continues to work together in cooperative relationship. The Spirit plans, the Son speaks, and the Father judges. Their example is the basis for another practical principle of the Creation Ethic: *Work is relational.* This principle is especially important to our understanding of how our daily work is affected by sin. In the Garden of Eden, the nature of human relationships was established in three dimensions: between Adam and God; between Adam and Eve; and between Adam and nature. When these relationships are spiritually intact, they are characterized by a quality of interaction that is spiritual within itself. Adam's relationship with God was characterized by the quality of *worship;* his relationship with Eve, by the quality of *wedlock;* and his relationship to nature, by the quality of *work.* Note that each of these qualities has value within itself. Worship, wedlock, and work are intrinsically "good" and need no outside support to give them value.

WORK AND HUMAN RELATIONSHIPS

Immediately, God's intended meaning for work comes forward. *Work is one of the three vital dimensions in human relationships which are ordained by God.* Worship, wedlock, and work stand together in the Creation story. Later on, priority will be given to the relationship with God and other persons in the first and the greatest commandment, "And you shall love the Lord your God with all your heart, with all your soul, with all your mind, and with all your strength" and "You shall love your neighbor as yourself" (Mark 12:30-31). While these commandments do not mention work, they set the stage for the biblical priority that makes work more than just our relationship with nature. Work reflects our relationship with God and our neighbor as well. Therefore, we can advance to the principle that *our work relationships are integral to our human nature.* While worship, wedlock, and work have intrinsic value in themselves, they are not independent of each other.

Genesis implies that the quality of one affects the quality of the other. Just as our human personality of body, mind, and soul is one, our human relationships of worship, wedlock, and work are interrelated. Practical examples abound. How many times have you known persons who drop out of worship and get in trouble with their marriage? Perhaps more often, we recall persons whose marriage relationships are broken and then they drop out of worship. And this happens not just in a marriage. In organizational settings, I have noted that persons who cannot work together also find it difficult to worship together. For instance, faculty members who seem to carry a chip on their shoulder will find a thousand ways to avoid a communion service and, especially in the Methodist tradition, a "love feast" in which bread is broken between members of the body of Christ as a sign of forgiveness and love. If a critical attitude keeps us from celebration in worship, we are in trouble.

We see then that our *work relationships are also integral to our spirituality.* Before Adam and Eve sinned, the spiritual nature of their relationship with God, each other, and nature, was taken for granted. Once they sinned, however, they learned the meaning of alienation from God, each other, and nature. Significantly, God used their work relationship with nature to define the nature of sin as *alienation.* The earth became a curse; work became hard; and the birth of children became painful. Certainly, the alienation with nature seems complete. But this was just the beginning. Adam and Eve were also alienated from God. When they lost the naturalness of communion with God as a sign of their alienation, they hid themselves from His presence. We hear the sadness in God's call to His beloved, but fallen, creation, "Where are you?" The astounding fact is that Adam broke the relationship, but God initiated the search for reconciliation. His call, "Where are you?" is universal to all humankind across all ages.

Adam's alienation became complete when he turned

against Eve and blamed her for his sin. Then to excuse himself with God, he whined, "The woman tempted me to eat." Thus the stage was set for fractured marriages for all time to come. A current joke going around is that the hairstyles and clothes for men and women are so much alike that you can't tell which is husband and which is wife until one of them complains, "You never listen to me." That's the wife. And if it were Adam and Eve, the husband would be the one who retaliates, "It's your fault." Broken relationships also have a way of rippling through the generations. Adam's alienation from Eve created the climate in which hostility became aggravated between their sons, Cain and Abel, even to the point of murder.

While on our vacation at a lake cabin, my wife and I introduced ourselves to a neighbor, a young man in his early thirties. In turn, he introduced us to his fiancée, a slightly older woman. All seemed normal until we learned that we had come from the same city and she said, "We live just over the hill from you." Immediately, we understood that they were living together as an engaged couple. Then, out of their cabin bounded two teenage boys, who came up to their mom to be introduced to us. Of course, the mystery thickened and our curiosity took wings. So, for the next week, we watched the personal interaction among this "modern" family. The boys and their mother often huddled as a threesome to talk about their plans. When this happened, the boyfriend always sat apart, never entering the conversation and sometimes walking away. Once the boys were gone, the woman changed instantly from a solicitous mother to a seductive lover. Stranger yet, when the boyfriend did interact with her sons, he became a third teen-ager, playing with the boys and being scolded by the mother for foolish pranks.

After observing this pattern of relationships for a week, my wife and I wondered aloud, "What kind of family will they be after marriage?" Then projecting further into the future we asked, "What kind of model will the boys have for their marriages and their families?" The web of divorce, cohabitation, remarriage, and divided families is tangled indeed.

Alienation causes breaks in all of the relationships of life and these pass on from generation to generation. As children of Adam and Eve, we personally experience this truth. When sin alienated them from God, their worship turned to fear, their wedlock, turned to hostility, and their work turned to pain. Who of us has not known the same symptoms of our sin? Worship, wedlock and work represent our ideals; fear, hostility, and pain represent our sin.

Work, then, is not an afterthought to God. Quite the opposite. *Work is integral to human relationships with God, other persons, and physical nature.* What happens in our worship affects our work and our wedlock; what happens in our wedlock affects our worship and our work; and what happens in our work affects our worship and our wedlock. Each of us can supply our own illustrations. If something goes wrong at work, how many of us leave the problem on the job? If I try to hide my job frustrations from my wife with a fake smile and quick kiss, she will quietly ask, "Did you have a rough day at the office?" God also gets His share of my problems. Devotional time turns into a refuge from work rather than a preparation for work. More often than not, however, I find the resolution to my work problem in the wise counsel of my wife or the prayerful answer of God.

Right this minute I am praying for a colleague who is also a dear and loyal friend. When I called him this morning, his crisp answers and cool tone told me that something was wrong. At first I took the blame upon myself. But when I asked him if something was the matter, he told me of an undiagnosed pain in his stomach that troubled him. Later I talked with another colleague, who shared my concern about the change in our friend. He too had talked with him, and had found out that a combination of family and work crises over which he had no control had hit him all at once. A superior executive, an exemplary Christian, and a loving father felt exhausted, frustrated, and even alienated from his closest friends.

THE RELATIONSHIPS OF WORK

Work is more than a task to be done. It is a relationship that involves the totality of life. If work were just a task to be done, we could define its relationships functionally. Imagine a series of concentric circles with the *technical tasks* to be done in the smallest, center circle. From there draw a larger circle, which is labeled as the *collective effort* to be done in the company of other workers. A third circle, then, identifies the *economic system* in which the worker performs the task, whether it is capitalism, communism, socialism, or a mixture of systems. In the fourth and outer circle, the task is defined in the *historical setting* in which the work has been done in a given society, such as North America since Colonial times, or India since its independence.

Such a functional scheme for the relationships of work is far too sterile. The person seems to be lost as only a cog in a machine of technical tasks, collective efforts, economic systems, and historical settings. Not that these more impersonal relationships do not affect the individual worker. We have already noted the actual and potential negative aspects of history, economics, organizations, and technology upon the personality and character of the worker. To define the relationships of work functionally rather than personally only aggravates this issue.

The spirituality of work requires quite a different model. Begin with the person as *worker* in the center circle. Expand, then, to the next circle of *coworker relationships*, add *community relationships* in the next outer ring, and conclude with *church relationships* in the outer concentric circle. In one way or another, our daily work interacts with each of these relationships in a spiritual context.

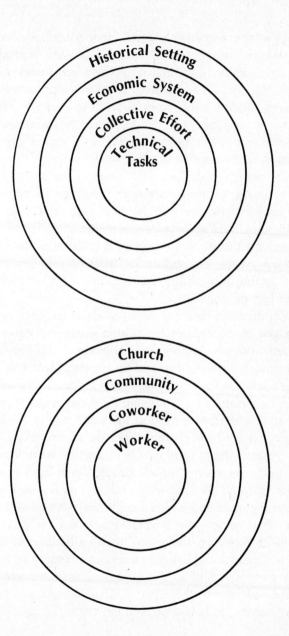

† As workers, we cannot avoid interpersonal relationships with *coworkers* on the job. The relationships may be vertical on a boss/employee level, horizontal on a coworker/coworker level, or even diagonal in what is called a *matrix* in which workers and even bosses change roles from project to project. Hi-tech companies, for instance, will let leadership be determined by the expertise required in a given project. In a "matrix" organization, today's leader may be tomorrow's follower.

On one given day recently, three of our children went through traumatic lessons in human relationships on the job and called home to talk about it. Douglas, our oldest son, got caught in a political trap in which contending forces in an administrative structure stalemated on a decision. Although the issue did not involve his work or his reputation, he became the frustrated victim of a vertical relationship to his superior over which he had no control.

On the same day, our youngest daughter, Sue, ran into the buzz saw of the matrix organization where she works. As a manager of women's clothing in a large store, she has to deal with her immediate supervisor and six buyers of women's clothing. In preparation for the annual sale, she worked until midnight sorting the stock and arranging the merchandise. Early the next morning when Sue arrived at the store, one of the buyers confronted her with the charge, "Your floor looks like a mess!" (You are spared the vulgarity.) Our daughter burst into tears and fled to the restroom. Her salespeople, however, heard what the buyer said and the one with seniority pushed the woman into a dressing room and "dressed her down" with equally strong language. Now it was the buyer's turn to flee in tears. Some minutes later, however, she returned with a bouquet of flowers for Sue, an admission of being wrong, and a request for forgiveness. As part of her plea, she confessed that she was under pressure to sell the clothes that she had bought and wanted them located in the best spot for high sales.

At the close of the same day, our youngest son, Rob, reported his first encounter with an irate mother of one of the teenagers on his summer tennis team. Due to a double booking in the main office, a group of mothers appeared on two different days for their tennis lessons at the same times our son was coaching their children. On the first occasion, Rob divided the time between the mothers and the children, but the second time he had already scheduled private lessons. Like a wounded tigress, one of the mothers verbally pounced on him and dug in her claws with the accusation that he was shortchanging her daughter in favor of private lessons. A nonviolent, "people" person, our son tried to explain that the front office set the schedule for him. Still, to make up for the double booking, he offered to give the mothers' class extra time. The mother would not be satisfied and stalked away with the threat to pull her daughter off Rob's tennis team which had a key competitive match the following day. Although the girl did appear for the match, she came with orders from her mother to play first so that the family could get away for their weekend. Obviously, the mother wanted to extract a pound of flesh while admitting that she was wrong.

How should we as Christians relate to our bosses, co-workers, subordinates, customers, or constituents? Although each of us must establish our own pattern of interpersonal relationships, my experience leads me to these five working principles:

> Pray for them in daily devotions,
> Value them as persons created in the image of God,
> Love them unequivocally through conflict,
> Praise them for positive changes in attitude and constructive achievements in work,
> Lead them by example—quality of work, integrity of character, consistency of position, and joy of spirit.

Let's apply these principles to our daughter's encounter with her buyer. As hard as it may seem, she would have to commit the buyer to God in prayer before each working day. Flowers and forgiveness are not quite enough. Their relationship took a beating that day, and when the pressure for sales rises to fever pitch again, the old conflict can resurface. Yet, there is a positive side to their confrontation. They both understand how pressure can take them to the breaking point. Our daughter now knows how to pray for her buyer as well as for herself at work. Furthermore, her daily prayer can help her see the buyer as a person with special gifts as well as nagging needs. Imagine our daughter praying this way, "Help me, Lord, to value her as Your child, love her with Your love, and praise her with Your Spirit." Such an attitude will not make it necessary for our daughter to say, "I am a Christian." The buyer will want to know how and why she leads her staff and her buyers by the personal example of a joyous, caring spirit, as well as strong sales and good profits which come from her reputation for integrity with customers and fairness with her staff. These same principles apply to believers and nonbelievers alike.

† Our daily work also extends into *community relationships* as part of our spiritual obligation. When Christians counter the ethic of self-interest with a demonstration of self-giving for the moral good of the community of which they are part, they exercise an indisputable witness on the job. This brings up the question of whether our daily work is contributing to the moral good of the larger community. A construction worker on a new highway might well justify the job as a contribution to the community, while an apartment manager whose owner exploits the poor cannot. A politician who compromises principles for power must seriously question his role, while a police officer in a swat squad combating drug pushers might not. Every Christian needs to ask the question, "Am I contributing to the moral good of the larger community?" If the answer is yes, we should

continue to explore the potential of the job for community impact. If the answer is no, we should either find a way to make a contribution or change jobs.

Another option for Christians is to volunteer for community service, either on or off the job. United Way, the Red Cross, the Heart Association, Habitat for Humanity, drug prevention, and literacy programs are just a few examples of community agencies which depend on volunteers on the job to lead their campaigns. I believe Christians should be the first to volunteer. The impulse is in our history. Just before Governor John Winthrop led the Pilgrims ashore to found Massachusetts Bay Colony, he preached a sermon to them which focused the biblical vision for the moral community:

> We must delight in each other, make others'
> conditions our own, rejoice together, mourn
> together, labor and suffer together, always hav-
> ing before our eyes our community as members
> of the same body.

Even though centuries have passed and our society has leaned heavily to the secular side, Christians cannot give up the biblical vision of the moral community. At every turn, on and off the job, we should be seeking ways in which to renew the moral roots of our community in our generation. Even now, we are living on the borrowed spiritual capital of the past. Our forebears founded and sustained the moral foundation upon which we depend. For us, then, the question remains: "Will we revitalize these moral roots in our generation so that our children and grandchildren will inherit not just the rights we enjoy, but the moral and spiritual qualities of life upon which we depend?"

† The relationships of our daily work do not stop at our community. As Christians, our work is also tied to our *church*

relationships. Central to that relationship is our corporate worship, the formal expression of the body of Christ which we have already seen in direct relationship to our daily work. Even though this relationship is formal and highly structured, none of us can afford to neglect the scriptural admonition, "Not forsaking the assembling of ourselves together" (Hebrews 10:25). Nor can we ignore the other, less formal, expression of the body of Christ. Students of spiritual renewal find evidence of what they call *ecclesiola* and *ecclesia* whenever there is a revival in the church. By *ecclesiola* they mean smaller, informal bodies of believers within the larger, formal structure of the *ecclesia* or the corporate church. We need both the *ecclesiola* and the *ecclesia* in support of our daily work. Especially in small group settings, we find the relational climate in which we can be honest about the victories and defeats in our daily work. We can discover the biblical meaning of the diversity and development of our individual gifts. The genius of the body of Christ is its variety of gifts in which each member brings the skills and experiences of daily work into the seamless fabric and Spirit-guided design, which represents the will and kingdom of God on earth. We see that relational reality in Peter's inspired insight:

> As each one has received a gift, minister it to one another, as good stewards of the manifold grace of God. If anyone speaks, let him speak as the oracles of God. If anyone ministers, let him do it as with the ability which God supplies, that in all things God may be glorified through Jesus Christ, to whom belong the glory and the dominion forever and ever. Amen (1 Peter 4:10-11).

The practical outworking of Peter's admonition brought ancient observers of the early church into awesome wonder.

THIRD PRINCIPLE:
WORK IS RELATIONAL

Celsus simply could not understand how the new community of Christ chose its leaders: "Wool workers, cobblers, and fullers, the most illiterate and vulgar of mankind, became venerated as teachers." Celsus failed to understand how Jesus, presumably the illiterate and vulgar handyman of Nazareth, became the teacher whom scholars confessed as "Master."

Peter's ideal remains with us. In too many cases, the body of Christ is built upon the segregation of callings, deference to wealth, and leadership of the clergy. Despite the lessons of history, most of us still do not draw a direct line between our daily work and our contribution to the body of Christ. Yet, we cannot deny what God wants to teach us through the life of Stephen, the first Christian martyr. When the body of Christ first gathered as the Apostolic Church, Stephen offered his gift for waiting tables—a menial task to be sure. He also brought his reputation for practical wisdom and his experience of the Spirit-filled life (Acts 6:3). Quite appropriately then, the members of the body of Christ elected him to the position as a deacon—to wait on tables so that the apostles could give themselves totally to the ministry of the Word and prayer. On first reading, one would think that the early church espoused the split-world view of work that made preaching and prayer superior to waiting on tables. Not so. After performing his duty as a deacon, Stephen went into the temple to preach the resurrection of Christ in one of the most eloquent sermons of all time. His pungent preaching cost him his life, but not without showing us how the practical skills of daily work contributed to the body of Christ and how the New Testament church created a climate that brought the hidden gifts of its members to their full potential. The spirituality of our daily work will never be fully known or appreciated until we see that model demonstrated once again.

As part of our spirituality, then, *our daily work must be relational.* God, the Father, Son, and Holy Spirit, established the principle for us in the fellowship of work in Creation—each one doing the work that expressed His unique contribution to the Trinity. Naturally, God followed His own example in His human creation as He put Adam in relationship to Himself through worship, to Eve through wedlock, and to nature through work. By this act, God demonstrated that work is more than a technical task to be done; it is also a *relational activity that expresses the quality of our interaction with God, other persons, and physical nature.* Once we accept this truth, our daily work can never be separated from our spirituality or segregated from the totality of our lives. Rather, we will see it as a center from which we extend our spiritual witness to our coworkers, our community, and our church. If there is any place where the connection between our daily work and our spiritual growth needs attention, this is it.

SPIRITUAL REFLECTIONS ON OUR WORK AND PEOPLE

Let him who stole steal no longer, but rather let him labor, working with his hands what is good, that he may have something to give to him who has need.

Ephesians 4:28

A PROVOCATIVE QUESTION

How do you deal with conflict in your relationships with coworkers? Does resolution come most often and most quickly if you are patient or confrontational in your response? Does it make a difference if the conflict is with a Christian or a non-Christian? Do you have any unresolved conflicts with persons in your work? What does the Spirit of God prompt you to do?

A PRACTICAL EXERCISE

Put names and faces to the practice of praying for, valuing, loving, praising, and leading your coworkers. How does this change your situation? Your attitude?

A PERSONAL PRAYER

Loving Father, enlarge the view of my daily work to embrace with love all of the people with whom I work, especially those who are hard to like, much less love. Amen

SEVEN

FOURTH PRINCIPLE:
WORK IS DEVELOPMENTAL

I would finish hoeing my garden."
—Francis of Assisi,
when asked what he would do if
he were to die at sunset.

Neither Rome nor the world was built in a day. Why, we ask, did God speak a word to bring the universe into existence and then take six days to work out the details? The simplest answer is that something cannot be created out of nothing gradually; primary creation is always instantaneous. Once God had brought the world into being, however, He worked according to the principle of secondary creation: *to make something out of something*. It takes time and must be done in stages. By His example, God demonstrated the developmental nature of our daily work as partners with Him in the task of secondary creation. Four developmental principles are given to us in the Creation story.

> Creative work takes time,
> Creative work is done in discrete but interde-
> pendent stages,
> Creative work advances toward higher and more
> sophisticated levels of achievement,

Creative work comes to maturity when human
nature reflects the image of God.

Note these principles in action through the calendar of
God's working days:

First Day: light is divided from darkness to
make night and day,

Second Day: water is separated from waters to
make the sky,

Third Day: the sea is separated from the land
and vegetation is made,

Fourth Day: sun, moon, and stars are made to
mark seasons, years, and to govern day and
night,

Fifth Day: fish and fowl are made with the instruction to fill the earth,

Sixth Day: after the creation of animal life,
God created Adam in His image as representative of humankind. Adam is then given dominion over all creation, instructed to fill the
earth, tame it, and tend to it along with the
promise of sustenance from all living things.

By direct inference we see that our work is also *developmental*. As God laid the foundations of the universe through
primary creation, we can also anticipate foundational work to
do. As God took time to do His secondary creation in stages,
we too can see our daily work developing over time and in
interlocking stages. As God's creation progressed through advancing levels, we too can anticipate higher and more sophisticated levels of achievement. And as God crowned His work
with the creation of man in His own image, we too can anticipate the maturity of our work in fulfilling God's purpose for our

human nature in relationship to other persons—to love, serve, and glorify Him.

OUR FOUNDATIONAL WORK

When God created the heavens and the earth *ex nihilo,* "out of nothing," He laid the foundation for all of the rest of His creative work. We too have foundational work to do.

Our vocational foundation must have height, breadth, and depth. *Educational achievement* gives us the dimension in height; *career options* give us our breadth; and *spiritual disciplines* give us our depth.

† Our vocational height. Educational achievements are the building blocks for height in our vocational foundation. Literacy is the first block upon which to build. Only in recent years have we become adequately sensitized to the widespread evidence of illiteracy in our nation. As a resident of Kentucky, I was shocked by the news that twenty-five percent of the people in the counties just east of us are *functionally illiterate.* As a person who has taken reading for granted, I had to rework my assumptions to make literacy a cause to which I am committed as a Christian. On several occasions, I have met poets, artists, songsters, philosophers, and theologians of the hills whose genius lay dormant because of their reading handicap.

Other levels of illiteracy are also being uncovered. Survey after survey reinforces an alarming fact: despite being blessed with the most extensive educational system in the world, many Americans are *culturally illiterate.* A large number do not know the dates of the Civil War, the year of the signing of the Constitution, or the century in which Columbus discovered America. Even more alarming is the finding that well-schooled Americans, even Christians, are *a-literate.* They can read, but they don't. Whether the deficiency is illiteracy or a-literacy, a Christian's vocational foundation is weakened if the fundamentals of reading are missing. To answer God's call to vocation, Christians must know how to read, understand what they read, and cultivate a thirst for reading.

Closely aligned with a commitment to literacy is a love for learning. Whenever I counsel students on careers, I invoke an axiom which reinforces what we call our *second vocation:* to be called to the consecration and development of our gifts. Translated into foundation building for our calling, it means that we should rise as high in the educational system as our gifts will allow. There may be rare exceptions, but it is safe to say that we waste our spiritual gifts if we do not cultivate them. Just the other day, a student with unusual gifts for intellectual inquiry, social awareness, and interpersonal sensitivity came into the office to tell me he was dropping out of seminary to work because he had no focused future. I accepted his decision to drop out, but not without the caveat, "Build an educational base commensurate with your God-given gifts. Otherwise you will limit your options for the future and short-circuit the full potential which God has in mind for you." He thanked me and promised to build that base.

✝ Our vocational breadth. Our vocational foundation also needs breadth. Most of us cannot claim to have chosen a special career early in life from which we have never varied. Rather, we fit the typical pattern of changing fields of interest three or four times before we make our career choice, and then changing three or four more times in succeeding years. Yet, there is another brutal fact of life with which we must deal. As we move through our careers, the options tend to narrow down by age and opportunity. For one thing, in a rapidly changing world we have to retrain ourselves in order to move from field to field. Even then, there are limits to retraining—our background preparation, our economic status, and especially our competition.

Furthermore, our age and vocational identity begin to work against us. As we grow older and gain obligations, it is more difficult to take the risk that a career change often entails. More difficult yet is the identity we develop in a given field of work and the network of contacts we create. A career change that requires retraining, risk, and new networking is not easy, despite the success stories we read about "opening horizons" and "freedom from stress" for persons who make mid-career changes. Especially as we grow older, we empathize with the displaced worker who said, "I'm too young to die and too old to learn a new trade."

All of this is intended to emphasize the broad base of work-related experiences we need as part of our vocational foundation. Whether after-school or summer jobs, curricular or extracurricular activities, early career moves or lateral transfers, all lend breadth to our vocational foundation which opens up multiple options for our future. A working rule is, "The broader the base, the wider the options."

† Our vocational depth. Both the height of our achievements and the breadth of our career options need the counterbalancing depth of spiritual discipline. Otherwise, educational achievements can lead to pride and career options dissipate in wandering. Spiritual discipline in the Word of God and in prayer keeps us humble in spirit and focused in direction. Also, spiritual discipline builds in us the ethical convictions and moral character which become the integrity base for any career, religious or secular. God calls us to a depth of spiritual integrity that opens up the height of educational achievement and sets us free to explore the breadth of career options.

OUR VOCATIONAL STAGES

Just as God's work in Creation advanced through progressive but independent stages, so our long-term work plan should show the same progress. Imagine a pyramid of work built upon a strong vocational foundation.

VOCATIONAL STAGES

Figure #1

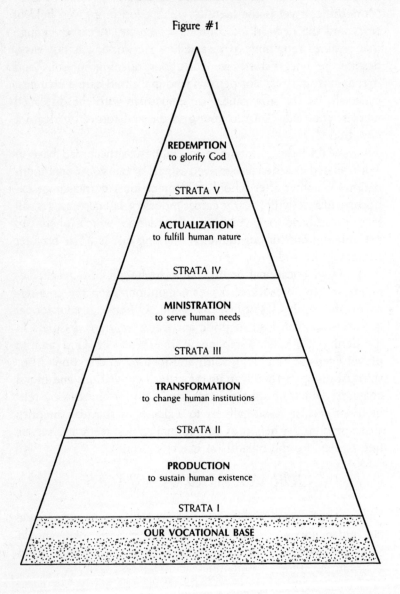

REDEMPTION
to glorify God

STRATA V

ACTUALIZATION
to fulfill human nature

STRATA IV

MINISTRATION
to serve human needs

STRATA III

TRANSFORMATION
to change human institutions

STRATA II

PRODUCTION
to sustain human existence

STRATA I

OUR VOCATIONAL BASE

FOURTH PRINCIPLE:
WORK IS DEVELOPMENTAL

✝ Strata I is *production: to sustain human existence.* The most elementary work of all is to sustain human existence. The idea that menial work at minimum pay, to provide food, clothing, and shelter, is less dignified than a better job at higher pay, to supply our wants rather than our needs, is a serious distortion of biblical vocation. Both Old and New Testament Scripture are clear and firm in giving dignity to the labor of the hands. First and foremost, then, God calls us to work in order to meet our subsistence needs. His call also extends to offering political, economic, and legal support for persons whose circumstances make it a struggle to earn a living wage. For instance, I have been involved in community service programs for single, working mothers. Because of early marriage and motherhood, many of them lack the skills to compete for jobs which pay above the minimum wage. Their disadvantage compounds because most of these jobs do not include the benefits of health insurance, sick pay, or retirement. These mothers suffer most when their children are sick, hungry, in makeshift day-care programs, or on the streets as "latchkey kids." They deserve not only our assistance in wages and benefits, but also our respect for their efforts to hold "life and limb" together.

✝ *Strata II is transformation: to change human structures.* All human institutions and systems are flawed and capable of improvement. Christians cannot be satisfied with just keeping those institutions and systems running in order to produce the goods and services to sustain human existence. As "brooders" over our work, we will envision ways to change the climate, improve the system, and even transform the institutions with which we are associated. This attitude is consistent with our "second job"—to work for change as well as subsistence. In modern management language, change agents within an organization are identified as *intrapreneurs,* in contrast with *entrepreneurs* who create change outside of established institutions. Christians can be either intrapreneurs or entrepreneurs in our vocational work. For most of us, whether we are change agents inside or outside our organization is a matter of gifts. Our secular society has put a premium on the visionary ventures of entrepreneurs even when their tactics push ethical margins. Donald Trump, for instance, draws mixed emotions of awe and hate for his entrepreneurial appetite that ingested Atlantic City gambling casinos and his extravagant lifestyle that includes a floating palace in the form of a yacht. But the greed of some does not mean that Christians cannot be entrepreneurs. If we look back on the advancing movements and enlarging horizons of the church throughout history, we see that spiritual entrepreneurs have led the way.

At the same time, not enough credit has been given to Christians who are intrapreneurs. Our fast-moving society tends to reward the flash in the pan ahead of the faithful person. God, however, puts a premium on faithfulness. In the Book of Revelation, we read, "Be faithful until death, and I will give you the crown of life" (Revelation 2:10).

Although intrapreneurial changes may not be as spectacular as the innovations of entrepreneurs, the results may be more substantive and lasting. Mainline churches, for instance, are in membership decline and in need of spiritual revival. Rather than staying within the church and working for change as intrapreneurs, many pastors are leaving the established denomination, becoming entrepreneurs, and founding their own churches. For the most part, they trade one set of problems for another. Somehow I feel as if we need to honor those clergy or laity who faithfully work for renewal within a denomination, as much or more than we honor those who leave for their independent achievements. Whichever the case may be for us, our single desire should be to hear God say, "Well done, good and faithful servant" (Matthew 25:21).

In Studs Terkel's book *Working*, he tells about the bus driver who greets a crowded bus load of grumpy commuters at the end of the workday with this greeting: "Welcome aboard.

Until you get where you are going, this is home. Let's enjoy our time together." In his own inimitable way, he is an intrapreneur who is creatively transforming one of the most routine, plodding, and impersonal of human systems—public transportation.

† Strata III is *ministration: to serve human needs.* Quickly we recognize that service to human needs is a common thread that runs through all levels of our work, whether producing goods and services for the subsistence needs of those to whom we are obligated, transforming structures for human betterment, or more directly ministering to human hurts. By spirit and heartbeat, a Christian never loses sight of human hurts as integral to his or her vocational calling. Not only will we Christians be sensitive to hurting people and responsive to their needs, but we will also rigorously avoid causing hurts by demeaning their humanity or devaluing their work. There is no exception. No matter how menial our job or how minimal our wage, we are called to be masters of ministration with rich rewards for our servanthood. Especially, we are reminded of our responsibility for the bound, the blind, the bruised, and the broken among us. As we found in a study of domestic violence in our community, the hurts do not know the boundaries of race, sex, age, social class, economic status, or church affiliation. Wherever we work and at whatever level, ministration is our ministry.

† Strata IV is *actualization: to fulfill human nature.* Certainly one of the goals of our daily work is to realize our potential as men and women created in the image of God. From a psychological standpoint, Abraham Maslow has made "self-actualization" the goal of human development in his well-known hierarchy of values. In a paper that shook up the psychological world, Maslow dared to identify the qualities of the self-actualized person. He said that these persons exemplify the two criteria of optimal mental health: the absence of significant inner problems and the "full use and exploitation of talents, capabilities . . . (and) potentiality."[1] Expanding these two criteria in detail,

Maslow ascribed these distinctive qualities to the self-actualized person:

> self-acceptance
> acceptance of others
> autonomy
> spontaneity
> aesthetic sensitivity
> frequent mystical and transcendent experiences
> democratic rather than autocratic style
> involvement in a cause outside oneself
> good-natured, kind humor
> earnest desire to improve humanity
> search for privacy
> detachment from trivia
> exemplary values by which one lives.[2]

Coming directly to the self-actualized person's attitude toward life and work, Maslow spoke of an "outpouring of creativity."[3]

In this sense, there can be creative shoemakers or carpenters or clerks. Whatever one does can be done with a certain attitude, a certain spirit that arises out of the nature of the person. One can even *see* creatively, as a child does.

As good as it sounds, Maslow's description of the self-actualized person is deficient in spiritual values, even though most of his distinctive qualities imply moral integrity and religious maturity. We need the redemptive power of Jesus Christ to make us His new creation and the indwelling presence of the Holy Spirit to lead us to our full human potential. Then, all of Maslow's qualities take on the transcendent dimension which the Apostle Paul identified as "Christ in us" (Colossians 1:27). Actualization for the Christian, can never be "self-actualization." Rather, it is "Christ-actualization." This is why Maslow's hierarchy of values is like a truncated pyramid. The apex is missing. And if we stop here in relating our daily work to our human development, we will lapse back into a self-fulfillment ethic which we have already seen to be carrying the seeds of its own destruction.

† Strata V is *redemption: to glorify God*. Of course, this level of work is the apex of our efforts. Yet we must not make the mistake of assuming that it is separate from the rest of the work or more spiritual than the lower levels. Because God created humankind in His own image, the redemption of human nature is the crowning glory of our work. And the task is not so exotic as we might make it. Redemption means to restore human nature to its intended purpose, namely the fulfillment of human potential in the image of God. To see men and women become fully human and whole again is our highest vocational calling and the greatest reward for our work.

I cannot forget that my spiritual heritage began at a workbench in a tool-and-die shop. Grandpa McKenna had the reputation as a rough-living free spirit with a genius for anything mechanical, from steam engines in railroad yards to precision lathes in a tool-and-die shop. His bench partner angered Grandpa because he hummed strange tunes as he worked and read a Bible during lunch breaks. At first, my grandfather ridiculed and cursed him, but to no avail. One day Grandpa's insatiable curiosity got the best of him, so he asked his coworker about his reading. Soon he was sneaking snatches of Scripture on his lunch break and asking his partner for an explanation. One day a packing box in the corner of the shop became an altar as Grandpa McKenna confessed his sins and trusted Christ for his redemption. From then on, he and his partner hummed hymns together and literally transformed a dingy tool-and-die shop into a sanctuary of the Spirit. Even more important, Grandpa McKenna stopped wandering, took his faith home, won the respect of his neighbors, and lived to hear his grandson preach his first sermons!! In his life, the strata of production, transformation, ministration, actualization, and redemption all came together in the fullness of life, or better yet, in the fulfillment of his human nature as created in the image of God.

OUR VOCATIONAL MATURITY

Along with the wholeness of our work in the pyramid of vocational development, we gain a maturity of *skills, experience,* and *intuition* as we labor over a period of time.

Every job has an opportunity for developing *skills.* When I worked for a building contractor during the summer of my college days, for instance, I didn't know much about pounding nails, digging holes, laying tile, and carrying bricks with efficiency. Unschooled laborers and apprentice carpenters prided themselves in the moments when they taught or taunted a college kid.

After almost thirty years as a president of a college, university, or seminary, I am equally amazed at how much I have learned and how much I have yet to learn. At one time or another I have had to acquire skills in curriculum, instruction, faculty development, accounting, financial development, public relations, space allocations, building construction, government relations, and student life. Most recently my "growing edge" for skills development is in strategic planning and investment portfolios. One of the arguments for heaven is becoming more real to me: I need heaven as a continuation of my learning experience where I can continue my work.

Speaking of *experience,* the value of what I have seen and done is becoming priceless. Rich memories and nostalgic stories are now a part of my life experience. Turning points, traumatic events, failures, and successes stand out in my mind. Particularly, I recall the decisions of choice that opened one door and closed another: from engineering to pastoral ministry; from pastoral ministry to psychology; from psychology to higher education; from public university to Christian college; from Christian college to Christian university; and from Christian university to the theological seminary. Behind the scenes of those choices are others which represent the roads not taken. Either by my choice or that of others, I did not follow my desire to pursue medicine, politics, or business; I was not chosen as an editor of a national magazine, the director of a multimillion dollar foundation, or Secretary of Education in the Cabinet of the President of the United States. Whether winning or losing, moving or staying, choosing or not being chosen, all of these experiences form a rich and varied fabric woven by the Spirit of God. All my experience complements the skills which have been sharpened by both incentive and demand.

Someplace between skill development and experiential learning in our work is a mystique of *intuition* which plays a larger and larger part in our vocational role as we grow older. Intuition is a "sixth sense" of decision-making that develops out of the broad perspective we often call "wisdom." Some part of intuition may be inherited as a gift to a right-brain person but, for the most part, intuition is a product of skills and experience which cannot be rushed. The older I get, the more intuitive I become in sensing human needs, driving to the root of problems, weighing the alternatives, anticipating the consequences, and making decisions.

Vocational maturity has a synergetic effect when advanced skills, experience, and intuition come together to make us efficient at all levels of our work and effective in achieving our most important work goals. Put in the context of our models for vocational development, it means that we will find the way to be productive, transformative, ministrative, actualizing, and redemptive in our daily work and thus follow our calling as men and women of God "thoroughly equipped for every good work" (2 Timothy 3:17).

SPIRITUAL REFLECTIONS ON OUR WORK AND GROWTH

> . . . always in every prayer of mine making request for you all with joy . . . being confident of this very thing, that He who has begun a good work in you will complete it until the day of Jesus Christ.
>
> Philippians 1:4-6

A PROVOCATIVE QUESTION

Think back over the past few years of your vocational career. What have been the most meaningful and satisfying experiences in your work? Did you learn more from your successes or your failures?

A PRACTICAL EXERCISE

Chart the developmental level of your work. Is your daily work at the level of: (1) Production; (2) Transformation; (3) Ministration; (4) Actualization; (5) Redemption? What experiences from your daily work illustrate each level of development?

A PERSONAL PRAYER

O ever-present God, teach me patience in doing my daily work so that I can build on the past, be effective in the present, and anticipate the future. Amen

EIGHT

FIFTH PRINCIPLE: WORK IS RHYTHMICAL

*I*f God in heaven rested on the seventh day, why on earth can't we?"

—Anonymous

Even though God enjoys the advantage of unlimited energy and inexhaustible resources for His Creation, He followed a daily cycle of work and reflection as well as a weekly cycle of work and rest. His purpose was to give us an example for the rhythm of work. If God chose to pace His work, reflection, and rest, do we not need a pattern that permits us to work, worship, rest, and play? Here again we are up against the truth about work that bears directly upon the quality of our spiritual life. To be spiritually whole, we must be vocationally balanced.

Work needs rhythm. Otherwise, it can be detrimental to the fulfillment of our human nature as created in the image of God and to the fullness of life as promised by Christ in His redemption. Because work is honorable, we can use it as our excuse to neglect the worship, rest, and recreation which are essential to spiritual balance.

The cycle is prefigured in physical nature when God divided the light from dark and set the sun, moon, and stars in place to govern the seasons of the earth. As the cycle of the seasons—summer, winter, spring, and fall—keeps physical nature in balance, the cycle of work, worship, rest, and play is intended to keep human nature in balance. A rhythm is also implied. As the writer of Ecclesiastes reminds us, "To everything there is a season, a time for every purpose under heaven" (Ecclesiastes 3:1). A poetic listing of the timely nature of human activity follows, ranging all the way from "a time to be born" to "a time to die" (3:2). Then we learn that the writer of Ecclesiastes specifically has work in mind when he asks, "What profit has the worker from that in which he labors?" (3:9) Answering his own question in terms that reach back to Creation and forward to Redemption, he says:

> I have seen the God-given task with which the sons of men are to be occupied. He has made everything beautiful in its time. Also He has put eternity in their hearts, except that no one can find out the work that God does from beginning to end. I know that there is nothing better for them than to rejoice, and to do good in their lives, and also that every man should eat and drink and enjoy the good of all his labor—it is the gift of God (3:10-13).

While the writer of Ecclesiastes relates the satisfaction of work with the cycle of the seasons, the rhythm of music seems to express the relationship even more meaningfully. Work, worship, rest, and play are melody and harmony, point and counterpoint in the musical composition of life. The interrelationship among the elements is so finely tuned that no part can get out of balance without breaking the rhythm or causing discord. So, if we overwork, overworship, overrest, or overplay, we upset the balance and rhythm of our God-given nature. At the same time we must acknowledge that there is no single musical score for all persons. The rhythm varies by individual, by age, and by situation. During my graduate study, for example, I worked effectively for hours into the night. Now in middle age, my most productive work time has shifted from night to morning. Likewise, my rest cycle has expanded from four to eight hours and my recreational rhythm now requires regularity to regain perspective, avoid the bulge in front and pain in back. Worship has also changed from the hit-and-miss episodes of my career-climbing days. Spiritual sustenance is now bread and butter, not appetizer or dessert.

Twenty-nine years ago I began my career in the college presidency—just a fresh-faced kid who had the dubious and short-lived distinction of being the youngest college president in the nation. At that time, the tenure of college presidents averaged a little over four years. The average has fluctuated dramatically through times of crisis and calm during the past twenty-nine years; but generally speaking, I would qualify as a senior survivor in this role.

People who see the college presidency as a task of high stress and low satisfaction often ask me, "How can you survive?" Their question betrays their bias. They might better ask, "How do you thrive?" I would answer two ways. First of all, I have found joy in doing the will of God. My tenure of twenty-nine years includes moves from a college to a university to a seminary. It all began, however, when I responded to God's call and made Christian higher education the focus of my ministry. While far from perfect and sometimes wavering, I have never turned back from that call. The ministry of administration is still my joy.

Complementing the joy of my calling is the rhythm of my life during the past twenty-nine years. As a graduate student, I read a study of genius. To my surprise and encouragement, I learned that persons who were identified as geniuses did not necessarily excel in intellectual aptitude. Rather, they exhibited two special abilities, one natural and the other learned. They had the natural ability to find creative solutions to common problems. But they learned how to work when they worked, play when they played, and they did not confuse the two. I was encouraged. Knowing that my intellectual ability did not qualify me as a genius, I decided to exercise the insight over which I had control. Throughout the past twenty-nine years as a president, with only a few lapses that got me in trouble, I have worked when I worked, played when I played, and rested when I rested. Productivity in my work and re-creation of my spirit have been my rewards.

I wish I could say that I worship when I worship. This is my failure. Work tends to violate my worship and I am the poorer for it. Yet, when I discipline myself to give full attention to the worship experience, even poor music and bad preaching do not rob me of some spiritually meaningful moment. I thrive doing the will of God when I sense that I am in sync with the rhythm of work, worship, rest, and play.

THE RHYTHM OF WORK

In the Genesis story, God's daily work preceded His evening reflection. Likewise, our work precedes our worship. Not that work is more important than worship. Rather, work sets the stage for our worship as the time when we reflect upon the meaning of our life and vocation in reference to the will of God. The point is that work is so basic to our existence that its "beat" sets the basic rhythm for our lives. A few years ago, we talked with half-envy about workaholics, for whom work had become an obsession. Generally speaking, we thought highly of a person who succeeded on the job but failed at family fun, games, and small talk. Today, overwork has been classified as an addiction with negative effects similar to other addictions such as drugs, sex, gambling, and violence. The problem with this viewpoint is that *addiction* has become a wastebasket word to collect everything from original sin to inherited weakness. Also, I suspect that the term addiction is loosely employed to increase the clientele for professional counseling. To qualify as an addiction, overwork would have to pass the three-D test—*dependency*, *denial*, and *debilitation*. This means that a person would be dependent upon work to cope with reality, deny that dependence, and show debilitating effects in the quality of work and life itself. Defined this way, work is not part of the rhythm of life but is, rather, the whole of life. Work addiction is an extreme form of spiritual disequilibrium and is, in fact, idolatry.

Nonetheless, work can be personally or socially debilitating without affecting the quality of work itself. One of the most successful men I know says, "I never learned to be a father." A woman whose career took her back and forth across the country confessed, "My children have always thought of me as coming or going, never as a fully present mother." A college president I know never slept through a full night. When he awakened in the morning, a notepad on his nightstand listed all of the things he had to do that day. A heart attack cut short his career. In each case, overwork upset the personal rhythm and interpersonal relationships of life.

Work and work-related activities such as getting ready in the morning, breaking for lunch, and commuting occupy eighty percent of our waking time. For executives, the percentage will rise to ninety percent! Sheer reality tells us two things: our work must be meaningful or we will be miserable. We must set aside inviolable time for worship, rest, and play or our work will make us zombies or idolaters.

THE RHYTHM OF WORSHIP

Work and worship sound harmonious notes in the rhythm of life. In work we are fulfilling God's commandment to be producers, caretakers, and masters of nature. The power is heady. Before long we can get the notion that we are independent of God's wisdom and will. Three fallacies of human achievement follow.

The first is the notion, *Progress is unlimited*. Quite in contrast with the cyclical view of human history which dominates the Eastern mind, our Western civilization entertains the notion that history is a straight line ever moving upward in human progress. Sooner or later, we will learn that progress is neither unlimited nor inevitable. Instead, the myth of Sisyphus will come true. Sisyphus was forever condemned to roll a stone toward the top of a mountain only to have it roll down to the bottom again just as he reached his destination. In so many fields of human progress, we are learning the meaning of Ralph Waldo Emerson's axiom, "Society never advances." Almost every step of progress has its trade-offs, some of which are evil.

Another fallacy is, *Whatever the human mind can conceive, it can create*. Behind this notion lies the assumption that creation is mechanistic and finite—capable of being conquered by the human mind. Given time, it is assumed that science will solve all of the mysteries of the universe—physical, mental, and spiritual.

Still another fallacy is the insistence, *Whatever can be done, must be done*. Presumably, human invention has a momentum which knows no moral boundaries. The nuclear bomb, for instance, is a classic example of an invention that should not have happened, even though it could be done. Under the compulsion of doing the possible, physicists who first triggered the atomic bomb ignored the calculation of mathematicians who reported that the explosion could set off a chain reaction that would destroy the atmospheric envelope around the earth upon which human life depends. Though they gambled and won, Robert Oppenheimer, father of the A-bomb, spoke apocalyptic truth when he witnessed the unleashed force and said, "Physicists have now known sin." Ahead of us lies the never-never land of bioengineering which will permit us to tamper with the genetic structure of human beings. Have we learned our lesson? Sooner or later, when the prospects for evil outweigh the good, a moral line must be drawn, and human invention must be stopped.

Worship is the only check-and-balance upon work which will save us from ourselves. In worship, we become *recipients of grace* rather than the producers of goods, *confessors of need* rather than controllers of nature, and *servants of God* rather than slaves of technology. Most significantly, in worship we enter the overwhelming presence of God, His greatness, and His goodness. Not that God is absent in our work. Quite the contrary. His presence hallows our work and we can learn to practice His presence even while on the job. The difference in worship is that our total and undivided attention is brought into God's overwhelming presence. Awe moves us to *wonder*, sin brings us to *confession*, grace leads us to *forgiveness*, and faith lifts us to a *love* that takes us back to the joyful service of God. Like the pulsating voices of an antiphonal choir, work calls us to worship and worship sends us to work.

THE RHYTHM OF REST

Why did God rest from His work on the seventh day? Several answers centering on the meaning of rest apply directly to us.

† Rest is a natural phase in the rhythm of all creation. Whether in the cosmic rhythms of the galaxies, the seasons of the earth, or the biorhythm of human nature, there are periods of rest. While baby-sitting with our grandchildren, I noted the natural rhythm of creation firsthand. Marshall is a high-energy five-year-old, who rises at dawn going full speed with total intensity and vivid imagination for his childhood projects. He has to be coaxed to eat and resists any interruption. Periodically he asks me if I approve of his work. Otherwise, he seems to

regard me as a part of the furniture—which he takes for granted. Only at bedtime will he let me into his world. We watch
the stars together and talk about mysteries beyond our bedroom
perch. Suddenly, I feel a head on my lap and get no answers to
my questions. Marshall is asleep, as totally at rest as he was
totally at his work. In the natural rhythm of his young and
uninhibited life, he rests as well as he works.

† Rest is the final act of Creation. We tend to think of the
seventh day as a cessation from creation. True, He stopped the
work cycle but did not stop the creative process. The word *rest*
in the Genesis story is a positive term which suggests the final
stage of creation when all other parts and products of God's
work, including human nature, come together in perfect harmony in relationship to God as the center of the universe, when
the morning stars sing together (Job 38:7). Just to write these
words helps me to better understand what Augustine meant
when he said, "Our souls are restless till they rest in Thee."
Deep within each of us is a homesickness for the harmony of all
creation with God in order that we might be "at rest."

† God set aside a day just for Himself. God didn't need
such a day, but we do. As always, God had us in mind when He
"rested" on the seventh day. We read in Genesis that "God
blessed the seventh day and sanctified it" (Genesis 2:3). In the
rhythm of Creation which makes rest natural to the life cycle,
God blessed the seventh day as a special gift to us and also
sanctified the day as a special time for Himself.

If God in heaven rested on the seventh day, why on
earth can't we? Much could be written about the relationship
between rest and keeping the seventh day holy. In fact, a case
could be made for the fact that the stress which is the bane of
our contemporary existence, the symptom on which clinical and
pastoral counseling thrives, and even the status symbol for high-
achieving Christians, derives directly from the failure to keep
holy to the Lord the seventh day and enjoy the blessing of His

rest. Every psychological theory of healing, every technique for therapy, every remedy for wellness, every religious cult has one attraction in common: to offer "rest" for our souls. Whatever the name may be—"harmony," "wholeness," "nirvana," "peace," or "perfection"—it is synonymous with "rest."

How, then, do we sort out the biblical meaning of *God's rest* from the promises of counseling and cults? As God's revelation unfolds, we see "rest" in Genesis becomes God's promise to the Children of Israel when He leads them out of the bondage of Egypt, through the Sinai Desert, and into the Promised Land where they will enter into His "rest." A sense of harmony with God's purpose and plan brings with it the promise of His peace and perspective as they honor Him and His holy day.

God's "rest" was extended again in the Mosaic Law when the Israelites were commanded to let the soil lie at "rest" from planting every seventh year. The commandment was far more than a symbolic use of the number seven. The soil needed rest for the restoration of nutrients depleted in six years of planting. Today, this same concept of "rest" is used in colleges and universities where professors are given a "sabbatical" every seventh year in order to advance their learning, restore their energies, and enable them to return renewed to teaching.

The Epistle to the Hebrews extends the analogy of God's "rest" one step further. Sabbatical rest, the historical promise to the Israelites, is now advanced to *soul rest* for those who believe in Jesus Christ. The writer to the Hebrews minces no words when reminding the reader that the Israelites who failed to reach God's "rest" in the Promised Land failed because of unbelief. Therefore, with the strongest words, the writer to the Hebrews says, "Let us therefore be diligent to enter that rest, lest anyone fall after the same example of disobedience" (4:11). For every Christian, there is a creative rest in which we are fully at peace with God and ourselves. In Wesleyan circles, this "soul rest" is called "holiness"—not a sinless perfection, but a wholeness of heart that is motivated by love.

We have come full cycle. In Genesis, God rested on the seventh day from His finished work in order to enter into *sabbatical rest* in harmony with His created world. Generously, then, He invited His people, the Children of Israel, into a *caravan rest* from the weariness of Egypt and the wilderness of Sinai, as they, by faith, entered the Promised Land. There, they learned the values of the *"sabbatical rest"* for their land and for themselves. The culmination, however, comes in Christ. As we believe in Him, not only are we made the new creation of God, but we enter into the *soul rest* of harmony with God and His holiness. Sin is incompatible with God's rest. Until we are reconciled with God through Jesus Christ, all of our striving for harmony, healing, and holiness will be fleeting moments followed by deeper emptiness and more desperate need.

We see, then, why rest is so essential to the rhythm of work. Far more than relief from our work, we need to set aside the Sabbath Day for recentering our souls in God and receiving the blessings of re-creative rest which He has reserved for us. God's rest includes worship, but there are many other ways we can bring body, mind, and spirit into harmony with Him. When we do, we will experience the peace of His presence.

Careful reading of the Creation story will show that there is no evening mentioned at the close of the seventh day. Some scholars suggest that after God finished His work, He continued His rest to this day as an open invitation to us. Yet, our work is not yet finished. Like my grandson, Marshall, when we fall asleep with the "sweet amen of peace" in God's rest, we rise to work again—refreshed and ready.

THE RHYTHM OF PLAY

Our spiritual rhythm is not complete without play. Contrary to our usual thoughts, play is not the opposite of work. Rather, it is an essential complement to work—another note of harmony. If *play* is defined as "a spontaneous activity with a satisfying end," we begin to understand how much we need play as a part of our lives. Yet, to come to that understanding, we must first get over some misconceptions. One is that God did not play, as part of His creative process. While it is true that play is not specifically mentioned in the Creation story, it is wrong to assume that God has no playfulness in Him. In the Book of Job, we are informed that God does some things for a special purpose and for specific results. But other things He does because of "His soul desires" (Job 23:13). Later in the Book of Job, God Himself challenges Job to think about the hippopotamus, a member of God's creation, who is deemed worthless for all practical purposes. Yet, God tells Job, "I created him along with you." What a blow to the idea that God has no playfulness in Him. With an animal as ludicrous as the hippopotamus, He is telling us about an area of His creative activity that is spontaneous, free-ranging, and measured not by its usefulness but by His satisfaction.

Still, work and play are two separate realms. To expand our definition, play is spontaneous in action, free form in structure, venturesome in spirit, satisfying in outcome, and valuable in itself. Work, on the other hand, is a planned activity within a structured setting conducted according to preset rules, rewarded by compensation, and measured by production. In this contrast we can see the truth of the adage, "All work and no play makes Jack a dull boy." Play puts the spark into life. We all need regular times when we are free to be spontaneous, creative, imaginative, experimental, and adventuresome. One of my grandsons took me by the hand to show me the city he had built out of Lego blocks. Initially, he pointed out the buildings, streets, bridges, automobiles, trains, and planes. Then, after he peopled his city, his imagination set it in motion—cars moving, planes flying, doors opening, and children playing. With a healthy view of reality from his limited experience with cities, and with a fantasy that knew no bounds, he created the lively and joyful City of God all over again.

Play is not only for children. If Jack grows up to all work and no play, he will still be dull. Worse yet, he will be incomplete. Competitive sports and fitness programs will not do. By definition, they are more work than play. Competitive sports and fitness programs are planned, structured, regulated, and measured by the output of energy—another criterion for defining work.

We need an adult version of my grandson's play, with moments of free and spontaneous activity when imagination runs free, creative impulses are stimulated, and experience renews the spirit. For me, sailing is that kind of experience. Once I set my boat free from the dock and head into the wind, I change worlds. Quite in contrast with the highly structured, time-urgent, and goal-oriented nature of my executive work, sailing puts me at one with the wind—I go where it goes, move in its time, and find meaning in its motion. How well I remember the first time I experienced the exhilaration of being at one with the wind—sails filled to the slightest fluff, the hull leaning in perfect balance, and white water churning in the wake. That day I knew what Jesus meant when He used the analogy of the wind to describe the mystery of His new creation, "The wind blows where it wishes, and you hear the sound of it, but cannot tell where it comes from and where it goes. So is everyone who is born of the Spirit" (John 3:8). In thinking of God's redemptive action as His work, we may be missing God's redemptive play. Long before God put His plan of redemption into its "work" phase, we see His mind "at play," moving spontaneously over options, imagining the creation of a good world, struggling with the risk of human freedom, reacting against the thoughts of sacrificing His Son, and yet foreseeing the time when human redemption would be a reality. Dante had it right when he called the drama of redemption "the Divine Comedy." Redemption is "play" at its highest and best—God exercising the freedom of imagination weighing the options for action, foreseeing the risks of His choice, living with the divine/human paradox, and coming to the satisfying decision that He would send His Son to save the world. In rare moments, we too know how creative play leads to creative work. I find that the quality of my play directly affects the quality of my work. When I play well, I work better.

No two persons play in the same way. A garden may serve as well as a golf course, an art gallery as well as a book. Just as each of us must find the natural gift which becomes our work, the quiet sanctuary which leads us to worship and the holy time which gives us rest, so we must discover the kind of play which sets us free and satisfies our souls.

The rhythm of life has an integrity of its own. If we are to be whole in body, mind, and spirit, we need the balance of work, worship, rest, and play. In a washing machine, if the laundry is balanced, the machine works on a smooth whir. But if the load is out of balance, the thump of the cycle not only reduces the effectiveness of its operation, but can damage the machine itself. Likewise, if we have a thump in the rhythm of our work, worship, rest, and play cycles, the imbalance will begin to reduce our spiritual effectiveness and do long-term damage to our souls.

On the other hand, the naturally balanced rhythm of the work, worship, rest, and play cycle carries with it unlimited promise. Students of health and human behavior are preoccupied with the search for "wellness" as the total life concept in which physical, mental, and spiritual health are balanced for maximal enhancement of the person. The more the search goes on, however, the closer it comes to the transcendental and supernatural dimension that can only be fulfilled in Jesus Christ. When we come to that dimension, we dare not fall back upon faulty human solutions. One teacher of wellness, for instance, who is an evangelical Christian, brings a spiritual dimension to his theory, but permits "God" to be the Person revealed in the Scripture or *any identifiable object outside ourselves* which can serve as the centering force for our well-being. From there it is only a short step to the religious cults that prey upon our transcendental and supernatural needs, offering false solutions such as karma, godlikeness, and reincarnation.

Our prevention against therapeutic fads, substitute gods, and false cults is to hold fast to the truth that the fullness, balance and wholeness of life comes only through the person of Jesus Christ. He and He alone can fulfill the promise "I have come that they may have life, and that they may have it more abundantly" (John 10:10).

FROM DOING TO BEING

Jesus' promise of abundant living takes us back to another meaning of God's rest on the seventh day of Creation. It is a mistake to assume that the creative process was limited to six days followed by inactivity on the seventh day. Such an assumption misses the full meaning of the word *rest* and does injustice to the character of God. When He rested on the seventh day, God moved from *doing* to *being* and entered into creative rest. Note again that there is no evening for the seventh day.

Profound truth follows these insights into Scripture. First of all, *on the seventh day God entered into "creative rest."* He did not become the great watchmaker of the Deists who claim that God created the watch, started it, and then left it to run itself. Such a view is contrary to everything we know about the character of God. Rather, we believe that creation continues on the seventh day with God assuming a different, but not an *indifferent*, role.

Second, *the nature of God's creative rest is to move from "doing"* to "*being*." After the six days of creative "doing," God surveys His work and pronounces it "very good." For the moment, at least, the "doing" is over and the "being" begins. What, then, is the creative nature of God's "being" on the seventh day? There is no mystery. On the seventh day, God sets His humanity free for creative "doing" with the assurance of His creative "being"— expressed in His unfailing presence, His unconditional love and His unmerited grace.

As the father of an "empty nest," I think I understand a bit of the difference between God's "doing" and "being." Until the time that our children went to college and got married, I functioned as their "doing" father, providing for their needs, guiding their behavior, and monitoring their progress. Then the time came when love required that I set them free to become their own persons. Now, as I have told each of them, I cannot control them or make decisions for them; but I can assure them of my unfailing love in any circumstances, my immediate presence if they need me, and my willingness to give them everything I have if it would save them from disaster. Without setting myself up as the godly model, I join with every parent who knows what it means to move from the sixth day to the seventh day in relationship with my children. In a similar context, I also understand how God sent His own Son to redeem us when we rebelled against Him. Out of the "being" of my love, I would risk all I have to save one of my children, even if he or she had rejected me.

In this climate of God's presence, love, and grace, then, we come to our third insight into the meaning of "creative rest." *There is no evening on the seventh day because we are still living in that day.* This awareness offers inestimable meaning to our daily work. If we are in the seventh day of God's "creative rest," we as Christians are copartners with God in the continuation of His creation. While such a thought may overwhelm us at first, our second thought is to realize how worthy we are as persons in the mind of God and how important is our daily work in continuing His creation. God has given us the freedom to reject Him as our competitor and work for our own selfish ends, or to recognize Him as our God and work for His glory. In a very real sense, the seventh day belongs to us.

Abundant evidence from Scripture supports the "creative rest" of God on the seventh day. His unfailing presence was assured when God gave His promise to Jacob for all the generations of His people: "Behold, I am with you and will keep you wherever you go, and will bring you back to this land; for I will not leave you until I have done what I have spoken to you" (Genesis 28:15).

Our family, now scattered over thousands of miles across the United States, counts on that same promise of God's presence. If you come into the family room of what our children call "Our Ol' Kentucky Home," the President's home at Asbury Theological Seminary, you will see a Bible open to Psalm 121. We claim God's promise in the Scripture as the "McKenna Psalm" which has been handed down through four generations now. Each time that our family comes together we reclaim the promise: "The Lord shall preserve your going out and your coming in from this time forth, and even forevermore" (Psalm 121:8).

God's promise of His presence is backed up by His unconditional love. While that love comes to its fullest expression in the self-sacrifice of Jesus Christ, its promise is not absent between the time of Creation and Redemption. In the most difficult days of my career, I have often drawn upon the inspiration of the Prophet Jeremiah when he told of the Lord appearing to His people in the past with the promise: "I have loved you with an everlasting love; therefore with lovingkindness I have drawn you" (Jeremiah 31:3).

Then, in my most frustrating days when I have lost out on key appointments to which I have aspired, Jeremiah has again been my prophet: "For I know the thoughts that I think toward you, says the Lord, thoughts of peace and not of evil, to give you a future and a hope" (Jeremiah 29:11).

Who can doubt that God's movement from "doing" to "being" on the seventh day expressed His "creative rest"? Who can doubt that we go to our daily work in the promise of His unfailing presence and within the plans of His unconditional love?

But what a trust God puts in us. When He entered into His rest on the seventh day, God took the risk and set us free. Our freedom to make moral choices for good or evil and to do work that is creative or destructive is primary proof of our creation in the image of God. From the very beginning, God gave us our freedom when He put Adam in the Garden of Eden and said to him: "Of every tree of the garden you may freely eat; but of the tree of the knowledge of good and evil you shall not eat, for in the day that you eat of it you shall surely die" (Genesis 2:16-17).

All of human history is encompassed in the seventh day, a day without an evening. God is still at "creative rest," creating a climate for our daily work, setting us free to make our own decisions, assuring us of His unfailing presence, forgiving us when we fail, and showing His unconditional love by being personally interested in everything we do. His "being" is the hope for our "doing."

✝

SPIRITUAL REFLECTIONS
ON OUR WORK AND RHYTHM

Then God blessed the seventh day and
sanctified it, because in it He rested from all
His work which God had created and made.

Genesis 2:3

A PROVOCATIVE QUESTION

Do you feel trapped in an unnatural and imbalanced cycle of work,
worship, rest, and play? What do you need to do to escape the trap
and restore the rhythm?

A PRACTICAL EXERCISE

Assume that you have just received word that beginning tomorrow
morning you will be given a full year, fully financed, with your family
cared for, to do something you have always wanted to do. What
would you choose? What does your choice tell you about yourself and
the rhythm of your life?

A PERSONAL PRAYER

God of rhythm and beauty, help me to worship when I worship, work
when I work, rest when I rest, play when I play—and never get them
confused. Amen

NINE

SIXTH PRINCIPLE:
WORK IS MEANINGFUL

If it were desired to reduce
a man to nothing, it would be
necessary only to give his work
a character of uselessness."
—Fyodor Dostoevski

Sooner or later all work must come to an end. Perhaps it is the completion of a small task that takes just a few minutes; perhaps it is the closing of one job and the opening of another; perhaps it is the end of a career and the beginning of retirement; or perhaps it is the time when we stand before God and He judges us according to our works (Matthew 16:27).

Whenever work comes to an end, it is time to pass judgment on the results. We may be surprised to learn how vigorously and how regularly God judged the value of His work in the Creation. From the very first day when He separated the light from the darkness, God stepped back, surveyed His work and saw "that it was good" (Genesis 1:4).

His daily assessment continued on the second day when He divided the land from the sea (1:9); the third day when He produced vegetation (1:12); the fourth day when He made the sun, moon, and stars (1:18); the fifth day when He fashioned fish and fowl (1:21). On the sixth day, then, He stopped in the middle of the day to check the results of the quality of the animals He made before moving on to the crowning glory of His work—the formation of humankind in His own image (1:27). After this highest level of His Creation, God stepped back one more time and viewed His total work through the eyes of His perfection. What He saw prompted Him to declare, "it was *very* good" (1:31).

EVALUATING OUR WORK

In Scripture we find some fundamental principles about evaluating our work. God expects work to be evaluated. By setting the requirement for Himself, God dispels forever the idea that the performance of anyone is exempt from evaluation. And with evaluation comes accountability. One of the weakest and most pathetic excuses from a television evangelist caught in scandal was his plea, "I am responsible only to God." He is right in one way. God will be the final judge of his works, but he was failing to accept the Scripture he claimed to preach. Throughout biblical history God held His people accountable for their works, not only to Himself but to each other as well.

† God expects work to be evaluated in process, as well as in the finished product. By putting Himself on the line for a daily evaluation, God set the standard for review of our work during its developmental stages. We learn this lesson the hard way. When I made my first model airplane, my anticipation for the finished product caused me to start with Step I of the instructions and then skip over the details for Steps II, III, IV, and V. At Step VI disaster struck. Although the fuselage looked complete, I discovered that I had missed a step from which there was no recovery except to cut apart the thin balsa strips which formed the skeleton, and try to reglue them. I ruined that airplane but learned a lesson: *follow the instructions, and after each*

step, review your work before you move on.

Most of us are not subject to regular review of our work, and when we are, we tend to resist it. Yet, deep down, we know that it is best for us. Constructive criticism keeps both production and quality on the growing edge. Note the words *constructive* and *criticism.* In his book, *The One Minute Manager,* Kenneth Blanchard reminds us that review of our work should be guided by this goal: *change the behavior, but save the person.* Whether we are an employer giving the criticism or an employee receiving it, we must insist on saving the person. If I were an employee who suffered from personalized criticism of my work to the damage of my self-esteem, I would have to confront my boss. Sure, some bosses will not change, but others can learn that there is another way. In fact, as a Christian I would try to find a way to affirm my boss as a valued person. The surprise might be enough to encourage a change of attitude and behavior.

† God also expects a review of our finished work. The standard of judgment now steps up a notch. Not only must each part of our work be "good" but the finished product must be "very good" because all of the parts fit together. Throughout my career in Christian higher education, I have watched college presidents come to their positions as specialists in an area of work, such as academics, fund-raising, or student affairs. During their tenure as president they receive commendation for their work; but after they leave, the flaws of neglected programs are exposed. While the work of their presidencies might be judged "good" in part, it could not be considered "very good" in whole.

Or, take another example. Currently, my automobile is one of the "talking cars" that were a fad a few years ago. My grandchildren in particular will coax me to go through the whole routine of the voice saying, "Please fasten your seat belts." "Don't forget your keys." "A door is ajar." In fact, the older ones quickly caught the play on words and asked, "How can a door be a jar?" As exotic as it may seem, the computerized voice is a pain; somewhere in my car there is an intermittent electrical short that mechanics have not been able to find in four years of searching. Because of the flaw, the battery runs down, the speedometer quits working, and the voice goes silent. If you ask me how I evaluate my car, the answer is "good" but not "very good." All of the essential parts appear to be satisfactory, but the finished product is flawed.

God expects us to finish our work at a quality level which can be evaluated as "very good." Some of us are *innovators* with the genius to generate ideas and get things started. Others of us are *planners* with special ability for organizing ideas, establishing programs, developing work schedules to get things done. Still others are *implementers* or *doers* with the hands-on skills to turn plans into productive results. Whichever gift is ours, we need to finish our work in relationship to those with complementary gifts and labors. Innovators, planners, and implementers need each other. The Apostle Paul recognized this unity even in the ministry when he wrote, "I planted, Apollos watered, but God gave the increase" (1 Corinthians 3:6).

We each need to know where we fit in in the process, for few of us can bring our work to its final completion. We may finish products or come to closure on phases of our work, but as Christians we are always working by faith toward the end where God's total purpose is fulfilled on earth as it is in heaven. This perspective is especially necessary for those of us who do not see the result of our work. In education, for instance, our products are never finished. Even though we confer diplomas or degrees of completion upon our graduates, we use the word *commencement* to mark the occasion. Our goal is to prepare the student with the basic knowledge, values, and skills that can develop through a lifetime. More likely than not, we will never see the finished product. Occasionally, when we do, our joy is immeasurable. One of my former students has become a prominent Christian author. Each new book he writes reminds me of the time that we knelt together at an altar of prayer, where he struggled with the will of God for his life. I remember saying, "God has given you the gift of writing which He wants to use." Whether my former student remembers those words or not is incidental. When I read his gifted writings, I feel personal satisfaction in the finished product.

THE TEST OF QUALITY

God expects our work to pass the quality test for results that are "good" and "very good." The test comes in three questions:

† Is our work excellent? *Excellence* is an overused and misused word. Several years ago John Gardner wrote a book called *Excellence* that became one of the most significant influences upon my career in education. Most of us remember Gardner's quotation which has become part of our contemporary wisdom, "We must have excellent plumbers as well as philosophers; otherwise neither our pipes nor our philosophies will hold water."[2] We are told that Americans have the genius for creative new technology, but that the Japanese have the genius for quality by which they copy our technology and beat us at our own game by adding the highest level of quality to the product. The prediction for the future is clear. Unless Americans can add quality to creativity, our economy may collapse.

Early on my father taught me, "Any work worth doing is worth doing well." Later in life the standard has taken on a spiritual dimension for me. I am convinced that the excellence of our work is second only to the integrity of our character as the front edge of our Christian witness in the world. My sister, Pat, is a leading teacher and author in the field of business education. In preparation for the college classes she teaches on business writing, she collects letters that come to her and uses them as good and bad examples of style, content, and tone.

The other day she called me to report that she had received her first "perfect" letter, but that she couldn't use it in her class. Why? The letter came from Asbury Theological Seminary acknowledging a gift she had given to our ministry. The personal nature of the letter and its spiritual language made it unwise to use it in a public setting. But Pat wanted me to know, so I called for a copy of the letter and sent a note of congratulations along with my gratitude to the Executive Director of Development who had written it and to his secretary who had typed it. Excellence carries its own witness.

Is our work excellent? Wherever we are and whatever we do, the quality of our work opens the way for our Christian witness. It is not that we strive for excellence just to witness. The quality of our work has its own reward in the satisfaction that we have done our best with the gifts God has given us. Nothing less is pleasing to Him or to us.

† Is our work ethical? Excellence in our work cannot be separated from our ethics. Only ethical work can be good. If our best efforts are not "right" in relationship to what is truthful and fair, our work is corrupted. In all aspects, our work must be true. I remember a contractor who was also a lay leader in his local church. In the community, however, he had the reputation for cutting the margins on the specifications on his buildings so that roofs with minimal tar leaked early and pipes with thin wrappings corroded before their time. Each time I heard him testify in church, I thought about leaky roofs and corroded pipes.

The ethic of truth will apply to the *process* of our work as well as to its *finished product*. Too many people have succumbed to the old falsehood that the end justifies the means. One of the most blatant current violations of truth is to justify state lotteries because the profits improve education. To justify the *means* of gambling for the *end* of education is unconscionable. Moral ends can never be reached by immoral means.

The same falsehood is also applied to fund-raising projects in religious organizations. One church held a walkathon for missions using its youth as the walkers. At the risk of being charged with an anti-missions attitude, I refused to contribute when I found out that the organization which the church called in to organize the walkathon would "walk off" with sixty percent of the contributions as administrative costs.

How far does truthfulness go? A founder of a national insurance corporation believes that it goes down to paper clips. He tells about an up-and-coming executive who was headed for the presidency of the company. When the founding chairman found that the executive kept his office at home supplied with boxes of company paper clips, he fired him. In retaliation, the executive set up a competitive company which had momentary success but ended up in bankruptcy when the agency which regulates the insurance industry found that he had falsified records from the start of the company. When the founding chairman begins his orientation sessions for new employees with the words, "Honesty begins with paper clips," everyone listens.

What is the minimal standard of truth against which to measure the *good* of our work? If we are public officials, it is our oath of office; if we are doctors or lawyers, it is our code of ethics; if we are clergy, it is our vow of ordination; if we are contracted employees, it is the terms of our agreement; if we are hourly workers, it is the stipulations for our hiring.

Over and above our oaths, vows, contracts, and verbal agreements is the spiritual standard for truthfulness revealed in the Word of God. Something more than a general morality is expected of Christians. For example, Jesus said, "Let your light so shine before men, that they may see your good works and glorify your Father in heaven" (Matthew 5:16). We usually interpret this passage as an admonition for our Christian witness. More careful reading shows that the brilliant light of our faith reveals our work to be so indisputably good that even nonbelievers glorify God. Imagine our daily work under such scrutiny. Unless our work is right, fair, and true, it cannot stand the test. The light of truth is like the investigative light of the media searching into the background of public officials. Not many years ago the escapades of politicians could be covered up. This morning's newspaper, for instance, carried another story about the cover-up of Chappaquiddick to protect the political future of Teddy Kennedy. Today we cannot imagine such a possibility. The media now uncovers every sin and flaw of our politicians, ranging from Joseph Biden's plagiarism of thesis content to Pat Robertson's fatherhood before marriage.

Would our daily work stand such microscopic scrutiny? From time to time, I ask myself: How have I used my time? How have I treated my people? How have I reported my expenses? How have I written my reports? How have I presented my credentials? My conclusion brings me full cycle back to the biblical truth: under the glaring light of public visibility and in anticipation of the unavoidable light of final judgment, we Christians need to be "squeaky clean" in our personal lives and utterly true in our daily work.

† Is our work edifying? Still a higher standard of the *good* for our daily work is to ask, "Is it edifying?" Just as we must ask if our daily work is ethical, we must also ask if it is morally uplifting. The test has two parts: Does our work contribute to the moral good of the larger community, particularly to the body of Christ? and Does our work glorify God?

Our daily work is corrupted by radical self-interest when it contributes only to ourselves rather than to our community or the body of Christ of which we are a part. Today, self-actualization and self-esteem are so pervasive in our culture that even students of Christian colleges and seminaries put a premium on them. Christians need to stop and ask, "How does my daily work contribute to the moral good of the community, especially to the community of faith?"

When we ask this question, our perspective on our daily work radically changes. Think again of the "perfect" letter from our Executive Director of Development. Rather than the typist seeing herself as an insignificant laborer in a necessary office routine, she asks how the content and quality of the letter contributes to the communication of the mission of the seminary. The worker on the auto assembly line feels pride in a quality product of transportation. Homemakers who feel left out of the "working" world are contributing to the stability of the family and society. Whatever our vocation, I am convinced that God does not call us into daily work that has no value beyond our own self-realization. We are too interdependent for that.

Let's take the question, "Is it edifying?" one step further. Our daily work should not only *contribute to the good of the community*, but should also *enrich the body of Christ*. Just as in Christ, there is no East or West, no Jew or Greek, no bond or free, so in vocation there is neither sacred nor secular, neither menial nor exalted work. Custodians, secretaries, salespersons, and truck drivers can contribute just as much to the community of faith as accountants, attorneys, physicians, and chief executives. I know a truck driver who found Christ at a yuppie church in the suburbs. Three marriages and alcoholism had almost ruined his life; but after he met Christ, he had a story to tell that gave hope to newcomers who were up and out.

How often I have said that the diverse gifts of the congregation represent the greatest untapped resource of the church. If only we would take an inventory of the gifts and match them with the needs of the church, we would dignify our daily work and multiply the potential outreach of the body of Christ in our daily work as well as in our congregational ministries.

All of this leads us to the enlarged spiritual meaning of *good* as the test for our daily work. Certainly God spoke more meaning into His assessment of Creation than that it was excellent, ethical, and edifying. His Spirit must have leaped for joy with the satisfaction of work well done.

As we look back upon our daily work we should sense the joy of satisfaction for a work well done. When we do, we can close each day with the prayer, "Thank You, God, for the joy of my daily work." When this is not the case, the agenda for another day should appear before us in the question, "What can I do tomorrow to make a difference in my work so that I can close the next day with a sense of joy?" I know that many days end in frustration. Yet, as we gain the perspective of the spirituality of good work, and envision its potential for glorifying God, we will find ourselves finishing more and more days with the prayer of thanksgiving for the joy of our daily work.

✝

SPIRITUAL REFLECTIONS ON OUR WORK AND MEANING

Whatever you do, work at it with all your heart, as working for the Lord, not for men, since you know that you will receive an inheritance from the Lord as a reward.

Colossians 3:23

A PROVOCATIVE QUESTION

What is the quality of your daily work? Do you see it as an offering to God in which you do your best?

A PRACTICAL EXERCISE

All work has its moral dilemmas when we must choose between right and wrong. What has been the most difficult choice you have had to make in your work experience? Was it a clear choice between right and wrong? Or did you have to choose between a lower and a higher good? How did you resolve your dilemma?

A PERSONAL PRAYER

Lord, at least on occasion, may I experience the greatest reward and the highest commendation for my daily work when I sense Your Spirit saying, "It is very good." Amen

---

TEN

OUR DAILY PRAYER: GIVE US OUR DAILY WORK

> Work is love made visible,
> And if you can't work with love,
> But only with distaste,
> It is better that you should
> leave your work
> And sit at the gate of the temple
> And take alms from the people
> Who work with joy."
>
> —Kahlil Gibran

God's Creation Ethic is the natural *ideal* for our daily work; Adam's fall into sin is the ongoing *reality* with which we must live; Christ's redemption is the promised *hope* that is still before us. Until we are redeemed, we cannot know the spiritual fullness of our daily work. But once redeemed, our daily work can be transformed into a vehicle of grace through which we hear the call of God, do the will of God, and give the glory to God.

But first we must deal with the truth that Christ's purpose is to redeem us as workers, and then transform our daily work into a gift for the glory of God and fulfill His promise of all things becoming new. New creatures precede new work in God's redemptive plan. With His new creation come changes in our character, motives, attitudes, values, and goals. It is literally true: "If anyone is in Christ, he is a new creation, old things have passed away; behold all things have become new" (2 Corinthians 5:17). This includes our daily work.

TRANSFORMING OUR DAILY WORK

Now that I look back upon my childhood in a small independent Tabernacle in Ypsilanti, Michigan, I can see clearly how new Christians created new work. A majority of our members had migrated from the Deep South to join the labor force in the North, building B-24 bombers for World War II. Even though most of the southern transplants were unskilled people who bore the burden of being called "hillbillies," they were a socially and spiritually needy group of people who responded to the mixture of bombastic preaching, high-spirited singing, and occasional shouting spells in the Tabernacle services. The primary pull toward faith, however, came from the personal witnessing of the members on the job who assured their coworkers on the assembly line of immediate acceptance in the Tabernacle family. So, they came by ones, twos, and families to the services and responded by the scores to the altar call which followed every sermon. With their conversions they gained dignity that gave them confidence as witnesses and workers. Prayer and praise meetings became the platform for their reports. Jim, a toothless and bald-headed converted alcoholic, lisped his miracle story about finding a steady job, recovering his family, and winning fellow-workers to Christ. Sadie, a Southern woman who had dropped out of high school, lost two marriages, and who likened herself to Mary Magdalene, came back the Sunday after her conversion with a new hairdo and a modest but comely dress, to tell how she now saw herself and her work in a school cafeteria as ministerial rather than menial.

The stories could go on and on, but Ellsworth stands out in my mind. From an impoverished home in Appalachia, he had never learned to read. After his conversion, however, he declared that he would learn to read the Bible. Each week he reported his progress—verses, chapters, books, a Testament, and finally the triumphal moment—he had read the Bible clear through! Then his native intelligence took wings. He brought amazing intuitive insights to the Scriptures. Soon, he started a Bible study during the breaks from building bombers and then he brought his converts to church with him. He demonstrated what C.S. Lewis said, "I never met a common man." Jim, Sadie, and Ellsworth are the unforgettable characters who taught me how new creatures in Christ, nurtured in a redemptive community, can live out the spirituality of their work.

CHRIST'S PRINCIPLES OF WORK

Even if the Bible said nothing whatsoever about the spirituality of our daily work, Christ's example would be enough. The fact that He was born into a working home, learned a trade, labored until He reached the age of thirty, and never denied His workman's title as a carpenter settles the issue. Jesus Christ advances the meaning of work from the natural gift of creation to the supernatural gift of grace. In His work as a carpenter, for instance, we see far more than the dignity of common labor. Through His work Jesus revealed His servant character and His redemptive destiny. And He taught work-related principles for personal, interpersonal, and functional relationships.

† His teaching about the *person* in relationship to work leads the way. If we survey Christ's preaching and teaching for specific statements regarding our daily work, we don't find many. His primary purpose is to redeem the person and teach

the principles of developing new citizens in the new kingdom. Therefore, He deals most directly with the relationships of the person to God and to other persons. The centerpiece of His teaching is the first and greatest commandment, "to love Him with all the heart, with all the understanding, with all the soul, and with all the strength, and to love one's neighbor as oneself" (Mark 12:33). The inescapable truth confronts us that the broken relationship between God and us, us and others, us and nature can be restored only by love.

Once again we see how work is integrally connected with worship and wedlock—which is representative of all human relationships. In order for us to fulfill the purpose of God's creation, love must be activated as the motive for our daily work, in a similar way as love gives meaning to our worship and our wedlock. It is no violation of Scripture, therefore, to say, "Love your neighbor, and love your work." Christ restores this triad of relationships in His redemption.

† The second kind of relationship to work which Jesus teaches by word and example is the *interpersonal*. To introduce love into human relationships is to appeal to grace. Within ourselves we have no power to heal the alienations caused by sin. It is through our repentance of sin and trust in Christ that we all receive grace—best defined as the unmerited favor of God—and are reconciled to God in worship, to others, and to nature in our daily work. In grace, however, far more than justification or even reconciliation is enacted. As recipients of Christ's grace, we come to our daily work with a spirit of thanksgiving for grace received. To demonstrate our gratitude for what Christ has done for us so freely, we see our working relationships in a totally new context. Jesus set that context in His kingdom principles:

> to show respect to every person regardless of
> status (1 Peter 2:17)

> to do simple chores without expecting special
> favor (Luke 17:7-10)
>
> to be ready for emergencies beyond the call of
> duty (Luke 10:25-33)
>
> to consider others better than ourselves (Romans 12:3)
>
> to have integrity that is better than an oath
> (Matthew 5:33-37)
>
> to forgive debtors and enemies (Matthew 5:43-48)
>
> to lay up treasure in heaven (Matthew 6:19-21)
>
> to be anxious about nothing (Matthew 6:25-34).

Because these kingdom principles apply to all human relationships, they create a climate of grace for our daily work.

Jesus illustrated the difference between a climate of justice and a climate of grace in His parable of the workers and their daily pay. Those who were employed at the beginning of the day and those who worked only one hour received the same wage. When the full-day workers cried, "Foul," the master explained that he had the power to do justice and to show grace. To me this emphasizes God's grace more than His sovereignty. Jesus is teaching us how God sees us in our work—not through the eyes of lock-step justice which requires pay commensurate with the work done, but through the eyes of grace, which gives us all the opportunity to receive full forgiveness and abundant life without regard to our longevity in service, our status in the system, or the amount of our productivity in achievement. In all of our work relationships, including those where there is competition or conflict, if we will stop to ask, "How would grace respond?" our daily work will be transformed.

† A third principle of grace which Jesus taught bears upon our *functional* relationships in daily work. Consistent with His early occupation as a carpenter and with the role He assumed in

His early ministry, Jesus defined servanthood as the proper role of His followers in whatever they did. To be a servant in the Spirit of Jesus Christ without grace is impossible. Try as we might, if we do not receive grace for our daily work, our self-interest will break through time and time again to spoil our witness and cause cynicism, hostility, domination, and to reach for self-glory. A servant of Jesus Christ is called to be totally dependent upon the will of God the sovereign Master, and on the grace of Jesus the model Servant. *To be a servant, then, is to obey the will of God, speak the word of God, do the work of God, and give the glory to God.* Grace then invokes the law of greatness for us in our daily work:

> Whoever desires to become great among you, let
> him be your servant. And whoever desires to be
> first among you, let him be your slave—just as the
> Son of Man did not come to be served, but to
> serve, and to give His life a ransom for many
> (Matthew 20:26-28).

When I think about the law of greatness in the lives of believers I have known, I see a company of humble servants leading bishops and superintendents, presidents and pastors, celebrities and stars, into the kingdom of heaven:

> Carl, a janitor who whistles while he mops, be-
> cause God has saved him from suicide.
> Billy, the deformed boy who drags himself to
> the altar every time the pastor prays.
> Mary, a retiree who honors her Lord by keeping
> fresh flowers around the church.
> Randy, the blind man who sees farther into
> faith than those of us with sight.
> Allen, the mechanical genius who serves his

Lord by fixing things no one else can fix.
Sally, the prominent pastor's wife who ministers
on her own in a thousand unsung ways.

Without pretense or pride, these friends are all servants of Christ in their daily work.

Recently I met two Christian leaders from behind the Iron Curtain. My Western naïveté caused me to wonder how they could be Christians under Communism. Surely, I thought, if they had not come to a crisis of conscience with their atheistic government, they had to be compromising their faith. How wrong I was. Within minutes after we opened our conversation, I realized that I had compromised my faith more under the subtle pressure of my comfortable capitalism than they had under a Communist goverment. Yet, by grace under pressure and genius for frustrating the system, they demonstrated to me what the Apostle Paul meant when he encouraged believers, slave or free, to be content with their circumstances and to live as under Christ, their ultimate Master (1 Corinthians 7:21). If only we could make the same truth operational in our daily work. Rather than suffering from the symptoms of stress because we fight against our work or our position, we can find the means of continuing the work of Christ as His friends wherever we are.

PAUL'S INSTRUCTIONS FOR DAILY WORK

The Apostle Paul built upon the redemptive principles of Jesus in his practical instructions to the new Christian churches. Although his admonitions applied to specific situations for living in the cultures of which they were a part, they also help us as we consider how to base our daily work on the principles of Jesus. As the nature of work changes and the work ethic evolves, we need the guidance of the Holy Spirit to develop biblical practices for our work.

LOVE YOUR WORK

As we look at Paul's admonitions on work, we find so much that we can only cite some key examples:

All work is an answer to God's calling (Ephesians 5:1-9).

Each person is given a gift and with it a task (Romans 12:6).

Each gift for work is spiritually discerned (1 Corinthians 2:12-14).

Each believer is free to remain on the job, slave or free (1 Corinthians 7:20).

Every job is done to the glory of God (Ephesians 6:19).

No work done to the Lord is futile (1 Corinthians 15:18).

We bring to our work the mind of Christ (1 Thessalonians 1:3).

God's will and work come together in our will and work (Philippians 2:12).

Each person has a different calling, but we all serve one Lord (1 Corinthians 12:5).

All human work is temporal (1 Corinthians 7:29-31).

Our motivation for work is in Christ (Philippians 7:8-13).

We are to be worthy of the vocation to which we are called (Ephesians 4:1).

We are not to be a financial burden on others (1 Thessalonians 2:9).

We must not chafe at our ministry (Philippians 2:14).

We are to obey our superiors without fear (Titus 2:9-10).

We accept instruction (Colossians 3:22-25).

We are to treat subordinates fairly (1 Timothy 6:11-19).

We are to avoid idleness, luxury, and mendicancy (2 Thessalonians 3:6-12).

Employers and employees are to treat each other fairly since Christ is the master of both (Ephesians 6:9).

We are to break contact with thieves (1 Corinthians 5:10).

We are to be aware of the transiency of wealth (2 Timothy 6:10).

Any honest work is dignifying (Titus 3:1).

In the unity of the body of Christ there is no distinction or honor (Colossians 3:11).

Whatever our work, our employer is Jesus Christ (Colossians 3:22-24).

Our work is thanksgiving (Colossians 3:17).

We are urged to mind our own business and work with our hands (1 Thessalonians 4:1).

We are to share from our work with those in need (Ephesians 4:28).

We are God's workmanship, created in Christ for good works (Ephesians 2:10).

All work is service to the Lord (Ephesians 6:5-8), and

Every job is a work of faith and a labor of love (1 Thessalonians 1:3).

These examples show clearly that Paul and Jesus both emphasized *the motive of love* for doing God's will and work; *the expression of grace* for dealing with persons in work relationships; and *the attitude of servanthood* for depending upon God, being accountable to Him, and giving Him the glory. If we put these biblical concepts into practice, our daily work can be transformed.

THE SERVANT'S PRAYER

Our search for redemptive work principles comes to conclusion in Jesus' Parable of the Talents. Each person in the parable is called to steward the resources of the Master. Each is given different gifts of talents, each is charged with the responsibility for making an investment that will bring those talents to their full potential, and each is accountable to the Master for the results of his stewardship.

Except for the unfaithful steward who buried his talents, the others received their master's commendation: "Well done, good and faithful servant; you were faithful over a few things, I will make you ruler over many things. Enter into the joy of your Lord" (Matthew 25:21).

In the commendation of the Master are the criteria for reviewing the spirituality of our daily work. When all is said and done, God expects our work to be "well done," and He expects us to be "good," and "faithful."

✝ "Well done" is the standard of excellence for our daily work. Over and over again, I have found that there is no substitute for excellence as the point of entry for our Christian witness. As a college, university, and seminary president, I have always faced the temptation of pressuring our children to excel in their academic work. When our first son was little, the young women in my wife's prayer group brought weekly reports on the progress of their children—who teethed, walked, talked, read and spelled first. Right then and there, I decided we should drop out of the rat race with our children. It has paid off. Each, with varying speeds of development, has risen to his or her own level without extra pressure from parents. Collision came only if they were performing below their level because of lack of effort. When our youngest son, for instance, dropped a full letter grade from a B to a C because he failed to turn in a paper, we had a father/son meeting on self-discipline and time management.

I believe that God expects us to perform at our highest level of capacity in our daily work. Whether we answer telephones, construct buildings, teach children, sell products, or preach, our goal should be to hear His commendation, "Well done."

† God's second expectation for our daily work enjoins the quality of our character with the quality of our performance in the commendation "good." The same standard which God applied to His own work of creation—"good"—involved two dimensions: the *holiness* of His character and the *wholeness* of His work. Our daily work is subject to the same twofold test. "Good" is the inner integrity or personal holiness that we bring to our labor, an integrity that can be fully known only through faith in Jesus Christ and the indwelling of His Holy Spirit. "Good" is also the wholeness of our completed task. It means that the quality of the job extends to the relational aspect with other coworkers, the moral community, and the body of Christ, as well as to our vocational competence. It is one thing to push a project through to completion, and quite another to leave a trail of exhausted people and questionable decisions along the way. The spirituality and the goodness of our daily work is proven by *the holiness of our character* and *the wholeness of our contribution.*

† "Faithfulness" is God's third expectation for our stewardship. To be faithful is to be consistent in our tasks and in our trust. Studies show that the trust of followers is built on the consistency of leaders. To accept the trust of talents and tasks which God has given us and then to hold our course through highs and lows, praise and criticisms, success and failure—this is the path of the faithful servant. The Apostle Paul went so far as to say, "But may the God of all grace, who called us to His eternal glory by Christ Jesus, after you have suffered a while, perfect, establish, strengthen, and settle you" (1 Peter 5:10).

As "good" is to be true to oneself, so "faithful" is to be

true to one's trust. The spirituality of our daily work is joined to the quality of our finished work in the same way that it is bound to the quality of our personal character.

† "Servant," in the Parable of the Talents, means "love-slave." Thus, a Christian servant at work is bonded to the will of God, and yet is free to develop the full potential of personhood through the investment and growth of God-given talents. Puritans had no corner on obedience, craftsmen had no hold on creativity, entrepreneurs have no exclusive right to risk, careerists have no special claim on enjoyment, and self-developers are not alone in their interest in personal growth. All of these opportunities belong to the Christian who lives and works by the biblical ethic. "Well done, good and faithful servant" is more than an eternal hope for our stewardship. It is a present possibility for our daily work.

But there is more. In the Creation Ethic we are copartners with God in secondary creation—making good things out of existing resources. By Christ's example, we are commanded to be servants who do God's will and God's work. By His grace, the value of our daily work rises to redemptive heights when we are called the *friends* of Christ.

> No longer do I call you servants, for a servant does not know what his master is doing; but I have called you friends, for all things that I have heard from My Father I have made known to you. You did not choose Me, but I chose you and appointed you that you should go and bear fruit, and that your fruit should remain, that whatever you ask the Father in My name He may give you.
>
> These things I command you, that you love one another.
>
> (John 15:15-17)

OUR DAILY PRAYER:
GIVE US OUR DAILY WORK

What confidence God has placed in us! His intention is that our daily work be a continuation of the redemptive work of Jesus Christ. Because love and grace converge in our daily work, no vocational track, career path, or current job is unworthy of a Christian. In a very real sense, we are the *friends* of Christ.

So let our prayer be, "LORD, GIVE US THIS DAY OUR DAILY WORK." To do the will of God as His vocational calling, with His gifts, by His grace, and for His glory, is to love our work—an experience of joy that awaits us all!

✝

SPIRITUAL REFLECTIONS ON OUR WORK AND LOVE

Remembering without ceasing your work of faith, labor of love, and patience of hope in our Lord Jesus Christ in the sight of our God and Father.

1 Thessalonians 1:3

A PROVOCATIVE QUESTION

What are the major temptations in your work which could keep you from being faithful? If your coworkers were asked if they could trust you because of your integrity and consistency, how do you think they would answer?

A PRACTICAL EXERCISE

Much is said about being a servant. If you were to rewrite your job description according to a servant role, what qualifications, expectations, tasks, and terms would you change and emphasize?

A PERSONAL PRAYER

Redeeming Christ, fill me with the joy of doing my daily work with faith, hope, and love—knowing that the greatest of these is love. Amen

FOR FURTHER READING

The following materials are suggested to help you increase your understanding of Spiritual Formation, and more importantly, to help you grow in your faith. Readings are categorized under basic headings having to do with our formation. Most of the books are in print at the time of this compilation. The few which are not can be obtained from most college and seminary libraries in your area. In addition to these resources, please use the footnotes as a further means of exploring the various topics developed in this book.

General Readings

1. Leslie Weatherhead, *The Transforming Friendship*
2. Steve Harper, *Devotional Life in the Wesleyan Tradition*
3. Maxie Dunnam, *Alive in Christ*
4. E. Stanley Jones, *The Way*
5. Henri Nouwen, *Making All Things New*
6. Evelyn Underhill, *The Spiritual Life*
7. Alan Jones & Rachel Homer, *Living in the Spirit*
8. Iris Cully, *Education for Spiritual Growth*
9. Benedict Groeschel, *Spiritual Passages*

Scripture

1. Robert Mulholland, *Shaped by the Word*
2. David Thompson, *Bible Study That Works*
3. Susan Muto, *A Guide to Spiritual Reading*
4. Thomas Merton, *Opening the Bible*
5. H. A. Nielsen, *The Bible As If for the First Time*

Prayer

1. Harry E. Fosdick, *The Meaning of Prayer*
2. Dick Eastman, *The Hour That Changes the World*
3. Kenneth Leech, *True Prayer*
4. Anthony Bloom, *Beginning to Pray*
5. Maxie Dunnam, *The Workbook of Living Prayer*
6. O. Hallesby, *Prayer*

The Lord's Supper

1. William Willimon, *Sunday Dinner*
2. William Barclay, *The Lord's Supper*
3. Martin Marty, *The Lord's Supper*

Fasting

1. Richard Foster, *Celebration of Discipline*
   (helpful chapter)
2. Tilden Edwards, *Living Simply Through the Day*
   (helpful chapter)

Direction/Accountability

1. David Watson, *Accountable Discipleship*
2. Tilden Edwards, *Spiritual Friend*
3. Kenneth Leech, *Soul Friend*
4. Robert Coleman, *The Master Plan of Evangelism*

Personality and Spiritual Development

1. David Keirsey, *Please Understand Me*
2. Harold Grant, *From Image to Likeness*
3. Christopher Bryant, *The River Within*
4. Chester Michael, *Prayer and Temperament*

The Holy Spirit

1. Billy Graham, *The Holy Spirit*
2. Kenneth Kinghorn, *The Gifts of the Spirit*

3. Myron Augsburger, *Quench Not the Spirit*

Discipline and Disciplines
1. Richard Foster, *Celebration of Discipline*
2. Gordon MacDonald, *Ordering Your Private World*
3. Albert E. Day, *Discipline and Discovery**
4. James Earl Massey, *Spiritual Disciplines*
5. Maxie Dunnam, *The Workbook of Spiritual Disciplines*

History of Christian Spirituality
1. Urban Holmes, *A History of Christian Spirituality*
2. Alan Jones & Rachel Hosmer, *Living in the Spirit* (helpful chapter)

Devotional Classics (Introduction to)
1. Tilden Edwards, *The Living Testament: The Essential Writings Since the New Testament*
2. Thomas Kepler, *An Anthology of Devotional Literature*
3. *The Upper Room Devotional Classics*
4. Paulist Press Series, *The Classics of Western Spirituality*

Social Spirituality
1. John Carmody, *Holistic Spirituality*
2. William Stringfellow, *The Politics of Spirituality*
3. Dietrich Bonhoeffer, *Life Together*
4. Thomas Kelly, *A Testament of Devotion* (helpful chapter)
5. Henri Nouwen, *Gracias!*
6. Henri Nouwen, *Compassion*

Ministry and Spiritual Formation
1. Edward Bratcher, *The Walk-on-Water Syndrome*
2. Henri Nouwen, *The Living Reminder*
3. Louis McBirney, *Every Pastor Needs a Pastor*

4. Henri Nouwen, *Creative Ministry*
5. Oswald Sanders, *Spiritual Leadership*

Devotional Guides and Prayer Books

1. Rueben Job, *The Upper Room Guide to Prayer for Ministers and Other Servants*
2. Bob Benson, *Disciplines for the Inner Life*
3. John Baille, *A Diary of Private Prayer*
4. Charles Swindoll, *Growing Strong in the Seasons of Life*
5. John Doberstein, *The Minister's Prayer Book*
6. *The Book of Common Prayer*

NOTES

Chapter One

1. Georgia Harkness, *The Dark Night of the Soul* (New York: Abingdon-Cokesbury Press, 1945). Title taken from quotation of St. John of the Cross.

2. Doug Sherman and William Hendricks, *Your Work Matters to God* (Colorado Springs: NavPress, 1987).

3. Studs Terkel, *Working* (New York: Pantheon Books, 1972), xi.

4. Ibid., xi-xii.

5. Ibid., xxiv.

6. Daniel Yankelovich, *New Rules: Living in a World Turned Upside Down* (New York: Random House, 1981), 9–10.

7. Robert Bellah, *Habits of the Heart: Individualism and Commitment in American Life* (New York: Harper and Row, 1986), 47.

Chapter Two

1. Gail Sheehy, *Character: America's Search for Leadership* (New York: Morrow, 1988).

2. Michael Maccoby, *The Leader* (New York: Simon and Schuster, 1981), 16.

3. James Davison Hunter, *Evangelicalism: The Coming Generation* (Chicago: The University of Chicago Press, 1987), 65–71.

4. Quoted in Harold C. Warlick, Jr., *Conquering Loneliness* (Waco, Texas: Word Books, 1979), 18.

Chapter Three

1. Maccoby, *Leader*, 39–54.

2. James McGregor Burns, *Leadership* (New York: Harper and Row, 1978).

3. C.S. Lewis, *The Screwtape Letters* and *Screwtape Proposes a Toast* (New York: The Macmillan Company, 1962), 156.

4. Yankelovich, *New Rules*, 8.

5. Maccoby, *Leader*, 41.

6. Ibid.

7. Dennis Jaffe, *Take This Job and Love It* (New York: Simon and Schuster, 1988).

8. Shirley Maclaine, *Dancing in the Light* (New York: Bantam, 1985), 133.

Chapter Four

1. Douglas LaBier, *Modern Madness: The Emotional Fallout of Success* (Reading, Mass.: Addison-Wesley Publishing Co., Inc., 1986), 26.

2. Ronni Sandroff, "Is Your Job Driving You Crazy?" *Psychology Today* (July/August 1989) 42–44.

3. Henri Nouwen, *Reaching Out* (Garden City, N.Y.: Image Books, 1986), 52.

Chapter Five

1. J.H. Oldham, *Work in Modern Society* (Richmond: John Knox Press, 1961), 49.

Chapter Six

1. Edward Hoffman, *The Right To Be Human: A Biography of Abraham Maslow* (Los Angeles: Jerry P. Tarcher, Inc., 1988), 157ff.

2. Ibid.

3. Ibid.

Chapter Nine

1. Kenneth Blanchard and Spencer Johnson, *The One Minute Manager* (New York: William Morrow & Co., Inc., 1982), 88.

2. John Gardner, *Excellence* (New York: Harper, 1961), 86.